HISTORY AND ANTIQUITIES

OF

TALLAGHT

IN THE COUNTY OF DUBLIN.

BY

WILLIAM DOMVILLE HANDCOCK, M.A.

SECOND EDITION

REVISED AND ENLARGED.

~~~~~~~~~

Anna Livia Press
Dublin

First published in1876
Revised and enlarged edition first published in 1899

This edition first published in 1991 by
Anna Livia Press Limited
5 Marine Road
Dún Laoghaire
County Dublin

ISBN: 1 871311 19 5

Cover by Bluett
Printed in Ireland by Colour Books Ltd.

PREFACE TO THE SECOND EDITION.

T the request of many friends, I venture to lay a
new edition of my uncle's HISTORY OF TALLAGHT
before the public. It is an unpretentious record, by one
who laid no claim to archæological knowledge of the
parish in which his family had long resided, and is not
free from the imperfections attendant on authorship
by one actively engaged in other pursuits. My uncle
was himself aware that the little work contained many
errors and omissions, and these he had intended to
correct and supply in a revised edition. With this
design he had made a number of notes; but unfortunately, as the greater portion of these were accidentally
destroyed after his death, only a few are now available.
In this edition I have made no avoidable alterations,
and have supplied such additional information as I have
been able to collect in foot-notes and appendices. My
warm thanks and grateful acknowledgments are due to
Mr. F. Elrington Ball, for very valuable aid in the
revision of this work, and for interesting notes which
he has supplied. To the Rev. William Reynell, B.D.,
I am indebted for much additional ecclesiastical information; and to Mr. Edward Blackburne, Q.C.;
Mr. M'Sweeny, of the Royal Irish Academy; and other
friends for kind assistance.

MARY BUTLER WHITE.

SALLY PARK,
    TEMPLEOGUE,

August, 1899.

PREFACE TO THE FIRST EDITION.

THE want of local history has often been complained of, and few writers care to describe what is passing around them ; yet, in after years, how interesting do such records become ! Old houses go to decay and their inhabitants die out ; in a comparatively short space of time no memory of either remains ; and if any inquiry becomes necessary, there is great difficulty in finding out anything about them. Within the last two hundred years, what changes have taken place in the topography of our County of Dublin : new roads, new boundaries, buildings, and plantations, have in many places altered the face of the country. Woods which covered large tracts have disappeared ; wastes and marshes have been reclaimed and drained ; hills formerly cultivated have again become covered with heath and furze, whilst others have been cleared and enclosed. How valuable would a History of the County of Dublin, such as D'Alton's, written two hundred years ago, be in the present day. D'Alton's is perhaps the only local History we have ; and although it contains inaccuracies, still it is a most valuable record.

Austin Cooper, about one hundred years ago, wrote descriptions and made accurate sketches of many old castles, churches, and other antiquities, not only in this county, but in other parts of Ireland. His manuscripts (for none of his writings were published) disappeared after his death, and for many years were lost ; but recently his grandson, who, with the same name, possesses similar tastes, by an advertisement in the London *Times*, obtained a clue which led to the discovery of a

large portion of them.   Many are still missing, but what
have been found are very interesting.[1]   Amongst the
unpublished MSS. of the Ordnance Survey, preserved
in the Royal Irish Academy, Professor O'Curry's Letters
describe many of the antiquities visited by him in 1837
in the parish of Tallaght.

There are many notices of Tallaght in *The Annals
of the Four Masters*, and *The Martyrology of Tallaght*
is among the earliest of our ecclesiastical MSS.   In
The Haliday Pamphlets may be found copies of *The
Templeogue Intelligencer*, the first number of which I
have given at length.   From these sources, and from
any others I could find, I have largely quoted.   Other
information has been obtained from inquiries amongst
old inhabitants, from notes of my grandfather, and from
recollections of my father, who has passed a long life in
this place, and remembers many anecdotes of times long
gone by.   Thus, by jotting down and stringing together
at odd times everything which I could discover about
Tallaght, I have formed the following History, which,
however imperfect, may some time hereafter be interesting to those who, like myself, are fond of old stories.
If any of his readers can give the author more information as to the localities mentioned, they would confer
a great obligation upon him.

WILLIAM DOMVILLE HANDCOCK.[2]

Sally Park, 1876.

---

[1] Austin Cooper, who was a Fellow of the Society of Antiquaries,
was Inspector of Military Barracks in Ireland. He resided at
Abbeyville House, near Malahide, built by the Right Hon. John
Beresford. He died in 1830, and was buried at Kinsaley. See
account of his works by Mr. E. R. M'C. Dix, in *The Irish
Builder* for 1897, p. 103.

[2] See Appendix A.

CONTENTS.

————+|+————

HISTORY OF TALLAGHT.

—⊢—

THE earliest notice we have of Taimhleacht, or Tallaght,[1] is in the account of the destruction of the colony of Parthalon by the first recorded plague or pestilence, related in *The Annals of the Four Masters* to have taken place in the year A.M. 2820. The entry by those annalists is: "Nine thousand of Parthalon's people died in one week, on Sean-mhagh-Ealta-Edair, viz., 5,000 men and 4,000 women, whence is named Taimhleacht Mhuin-tire-Parthaloin, now called Tallaght, near Dublin." The word "Tamh" means an epidemic pestilence; and the term "Taimhleacht" ("the plague monument"), which frequently enters into topographical names in Ireland, signifies a place where a number of persons cut off by pestilence were interred together.

This destruction of the colony of Parthalon, which is said to have occurred in Sean-mhagh-Ealta-Edair, or the old plain of the Valley of the Flocks, stretching

---

[1] Tallaght is an inland village and parish, in the barony of Uppercross, County Dublin, seven miles S.W. by W. from the G.P.O., Dublin, on the road to Blessington, comprising an area of 21,868 acres. There is a population of 4,921 in the parish, and 312 in the town, inhabiting 57 houses.

between Binn Edair (Howth) and Tallaght, on which
the city of Dublin now stands, is thus mentioned in
The Book of Invasions, contained in *The Book of
Leinster:*—" In Sean-mhagh-Edair, Parthalon became
extinct in 1,000 men and 4,000 women of one week's
mortality, or Tamh." This is the oldest manuscript
account of the pestilence we now possess.[1]

This Parthalon,[2] son of Sera, son of Sru, son of
Asruith, son of Braiment, son of Aithecta, son of
Magog, son of Japheth, son of Noah, slew his father and
mother in Greece, in order to obtain the crown, and to
deprive his eldest brother of the succession. He began
his voyage from Mygdonia, in Greece, and, steering by
Sicily, sailed on until he came into the Irish Sea. He
landed upon the 14th May, at a place called Inbhir
Scene,[3] in the west of Munster. His posterity continued in Ireland about 300 years, when the vengeance
of God overtook the offspring of the parricide, and the
whole number died, as mentioned, in a week at Binn
Edair, now called the Hill of Howth.

The great number of burial mounds, stone circles,
cairns, and other traces of an extensive place of interment of the earliest date on the Tallaght hills, would
seem to give some confirmation to this tradition.
Numbers of tombs, made with four rude stones, enclosing a square space, sometimes containing a cinerary urn,
and covered with a heavy, flat rock, have been, from
time to time, discovered. These tombs, called Kistvaens,

---

[1] See Report of the Census Commissioners, 1851, Pt. V, vol. i,
p. 41, and Blacker's *Sketches of Booterstown*, p. 59.

[2] Ruan, or Thuan, son of Parthalon, survived the plague, and is
said to have lived to the time of St. Patrick.

[3] The Kenmare River.

are a very old type of burial-place, and are found all over the world.

The next we find of Tallaght is in a very ancient Irish manuscript, at present preserved in the Burgundian Library at Brussels, called *The Martyrology of Tallaght*, a translation of which, by Eugene O'Curry, has been published. It was so called from having been compiled at the Monastery of Tallaght, or Tamlacht, by SS. Maelruain and Aengus, known as Aengus the Culdee.[1] It gives a long list of ecclesiastics. It is impossible to ascertain at what time a monastery was founded here ; but it is probable that in the reign of Donnchadh,[2] who ascended the throne of Ireland in 766, and reigned till 792, may be placed the foundation of the Abbey of Tamlacht, called Tamlactense Monasterium. The celebrated bishop, St. Maelruain, or Maelruan, as the name is sometimes spelled, rebuilt or enlarged the monastery. He was called "the Bright Sun of Ireland ;" and under his presidency peace, piety, and plenty prevailed throughout the ecclesiastical houses of this island.[3]

Aengus was a saint of the most exalted piety. He was called the Culdee, and sometimes Aengussius

[1] St. Aengus wrote also the History of the Old Testament in elegant metre.—Ware's *Writers of Ireland*, vol. i, p. 53.

[2] His son, Cellach, who died in 771, is said to have been buried at Tallaght.—*Annals of the Four Masters*.

[3] Bishop Reeves says that Donnchadh bestowed the site of Tamlacht on St. Maelruain, and that the first erection of Tamlacht Maelruain was in 769. A poem of St. Maelruain, in Irish, has been translated by Dr. O'Donovan.—Reeves, *On the Culdees*. Canon O'Hanlon says St. Maelruain belonged to a race who sprung from the seed of Heremon.—*Lives of the Irish Saints*.

The list of the folk of St. Maelruain will be found in Dr. Robert Atkinson's edition of *The Book of Leinster*, p. 370.

Hagiographus. From his infancy he devoted himself to a religious life, and to an extraordinary degree practised mortification. His progress in the paths of Christian sanctity, and his advancement in sacred learning, were so great that in a short time he bore the reputation of being one of the most pious and learned men of whom Ireland could boast. He retired to a cell which he had built, at a place still called Dysartenos, or "the Desert of Aengus," in the county of Limerick. Here, we are told, he was in the habit of making 300 genuflexions each day, and of repeating the entire Psalter, in three portions, the third while tied by the neck to a stake, with half his body plunged in a tub of cold water. The fame of such sanctity spread. Numbers flocked to his retreat, to enjoy the holy anchorite's conversation, and observe how he afflicted his unfortunate body. He was unable, therefore, to enjoy his penitential practices in peace. He secretly withdrew, and in course of time came to the monastery of St. Maelruain, at Tallaght, of the fame of which he had heard, and where his own repute was well known. He concealed his rank, and became a servant, in order that his vanity might be quenched. One day, while cutting wood, he chopped his left hand off; he stuck it on again, and it adhered all right, so great was the purity of his life. At length, being accidentally discovered by St. Maelruain, he was received by him with the warmest esteem and friendship, and soon after composed a metrical poem in the Irish language, known as *The Festilogium of St. Aengus*. It gives an account of the festivals observed in the Church in his time, and of the earlier saints and martyrs. In conjunction with St. Maelruain, he composed the work before mentioned as *The Martyrology of Tallaght*.

Full of good works, and in the odour of sanctity, St. Maelruain died on the 7th July, 792,[1] and his festival and a pattern at Tallaght were held annually on that day uninterruptedly for 1,082 years, being only abolished in 1874.[2] St. Aengus, finding his own end approaching, retired to the scene of his early devotions, and died there on Friday, 11th March, 824, one of the most celebrated of the early Irish saints. St. Maelruain's immediate successor was Airfhindan, or Airennan, "The Wise."

795. St. Joseph, Bishop of Tamlacht, died.

806. The descendants of Niall, King of Ireland, having violated the termon, or churchlands, of Tallaght, the monks took the bold step of seizing and retaining the chariot-horses of Aedh, the son of Niall, on the eve of the games which were annually celebrated at Tailltenn[3] in the County of Meath. His chariots, therefore, could

---

[1] " With a great and beautiful host,
  Parmenius' heavy troop,
  Maelruain ran to heaven,
  Splendid son of the Isle of the Gael."
                              —*Leabhar Breac.*

[2] There were also several remarkable days recorded for the Monastery of Tallaght, on which treasures or relics were acquired by its church. The bell of St. Tigearnach was long preserved there, and was, no doubt, used when solemn oaths were administered. It was considered the greatest profanation to swear falsely on a bell of the kind.

[3] Now Teltown, between Kells and Navan, on the Blackwater. The fair, which was periodically held there, was much frequented for the arrangement of marriages, and it was in conjunction with this fair that the games and sports took place. See *Dublin Penny Journal*, 1832, p. 127.

not run.   Aedh-Oirdnidhe for his violation afterwards
made a full atonement.

807. Eochaidh, Coarb of Tamlacht, died.

811. The Monastery devastated by the Danes.

823. Aedhan, Abbot of Tamlacht, died.

825. Echtghus, Coarb of Tamlacht, died.

863. Conmhal, Abbot of Tamlacht, died.

866. Daniel, Abbot of Gleann-da-locha and Tamlacht,
died.

868. Comhgan Foda, foster-son of Maelruain, died.

872. Torpaidh, Bishop and Scribe of Tamlacht, died.

873. Macoige, Abbot of Tamlacht, died.

889. Cochlan, Abbot of Teach-munna and Tamlacht,
died.

894. Leachnasach, Abbot of Tamlacht, died.

913. Scannlan, Bishop of Tamlacht, died.

937. Maeldomhnaigh, Abbot of Tamlacht, died.

938. Laidgnen, Coarb of Ferns and Tamlacht, died.

957. Martin, Bishop and Abbot of Tamlacht, died.

962. Cormac, Bishop of Tamlacht, died.

964. Crunnmhael, Bishop and Lector of Tamlacht,
died, being drowned in the Tochar.

966. Erc-Ua-Suailen, Bishop and Abbot of Tamlacht,
died.

1125. MacMaeilesuthain, of Tamlacht, died.

1179. Pope Alexander III confirmed Tallaght, with
its appurtenances, to the See of Dublin ; a grant which
Pope Innocent further ratified in 1216.[1]

1190. Laurence de Taulaght was Rector of Tallaght.

[1] The Archbishop's possessions centred round three leading
manors, Tallaght, Clondalkin, and Rathcoole, with Brittas dependent, and a minor detached group about Kilsantan in the Upper
Dodder Valley.—*Journal R. S. A. I.*, 1894, p. 163.

1216. By the Charter of Archbishop Comyn,[1] as confirmed by the Bull of Pope Celestius III, Tallaght, with its chapels[2] and parsonage house, was given to the then newly established Collegiate Church of St. Patrick's, in Dublin.

1220. About this year, Archbishop de Loundres,[3] being moved by the consideration that the principal dignitary of St. Patrick's Cathedral was subject to the greatest expense, with consent of the chapter, annexed to the deanery this church with the advowson of the vicarage, expectant on the resignation of Laurence de Tallagh, at that time rector, and further appropriated to that dignity a portion of moorland, near the Grange of Dean's Rath, for which the dean was to pay yearly at Easter one pound of frankincense to the Archbishop's chapel at Clondalkin.

1223. The Rector of Tallaght, as above arranged, resigned his church to the Dean of St. Patrick's.[4]

1226. Pope Gregory IX confirmed to the Dean of St. Patrick's the tithes, and the right of presentation to the vicarage of Tallaght,

1230. Archbishop Luke[5] further assured the church to the Dean, who continued to enjoy the presentation to the vicarage until it was lost to that dignitary by lapse.

[1] See notice of him in *Dictionary of National Biography*.

[2] The chapels of Killohan and St. Bridget. The former, situated in the townland of Old Bawn, has been waste since 1532 ; while the latter stood near the Dodder, and is likewise in ruins.— D'Alton's *History of County Dublin*.

[3] Henry de Loundres was Archbishop of Dublin, 1212-28. See notice of him in *Dictionary of National Biography*.

[4] William FitzGuido.

[5] Archbishop of Dublin, 1228-55. See Cotton's *Fasti Ecclesiae Hibernicae*.

1306. The vicarage of Tallaght was estimated at the annual value of five marks.

1324. Alexander de Bicknor,[1] Archbishop of Dublin, had a remission of money due by him, in consideration of his rebuilding Tallaght Castle, which work he accomplished; and from 1340 to 1821 Tallaght was a country residence of the Archbishops of Dublin.

1337. King Edward confirmed Tallaght to the See of Dublin,[2] as did King Richard in 1395.

1374. John Colton,[3] Vicar of St. Maelruain's, of Tallaght, was elevated to the Deanery of St. Patrick's, and subsequently became Primate.

1395. The King presented John Young to the Vicarage of Tallaght.

1403. The tithes of Tallaght parish were appropriated for the support of the Viceroy, Thomas Earl of Lancaster, son of Henry IV.[4]

1449. Michael Tregury, Archbishop of Dublin, repaired Tallaght Castle. He died on the 21st December, 1471, and was buried in St. Patrick's Cathedral, where his monument still remains.[5]

---

[1] Archbishop of Dublin, 1317-49. See notice of him in *Dictionary of National Biography*.

[2] Inspeximus by Edward III of King John's grants to See of Dublin. This Charter identifies Coillacht and its wood with Tallaght and Glenasmole.—Stokes's *Calendar of the Liber Niger Alani, Journal R. S. A. I.*, 1893.

[3] See Reeves's *Visitation of Archbishop Colton*, presented by him in 1850 to the Irish Archaeological Society.

[4] See mention of Tallaght in extracts from the "Roman Archives." —*Journal R. S. A. I.*, 1893, p. 134.

[5] See Introduction to *The Register of Wills and Inventories of the Diocese of Dublin*, 1457-83, edited for the R. S. A. I. by H. F. Berry, Esq.

1479. John Alleyn, Dean of St. Patrick's, demised to Simon Gower, Clerk, the Glebe of Tallaght Church for fifty-nine years, the lessee being bound to pay to the Dean eight silver pence yearly, and to build a house thereon of four couples, to keep the same stiff and staunch, and to make new ditches to the glebe.

1514. There is a letter from William Rokeby, then Archbishop of Dublin, to Cardinal Wolsey, dated from "Talaute" on December 14th in this year, preserved amongst the Irish State Papers.

1535. George Browne was Archbishop of Dublin, and several letters to Lord Cromwell and others on the state and religion of Ireland, were written at Tallaght; one, bearing date 16th February, 1539, contains the following lament :—" God knoweth what a treasure the King's Majesty and your Lordship have here of my Lord Chancellor, who is a right wise gentleman, and a judge very indifferent, and shifteth matters depending before him full briefly, to the great ease of the king's subjects, the poor suitors. And for my part, I may well account him to be my special friend, for during fourteen or fifteen days this Council time, I was his continual guest. Other place had I none to repair unto but only Tallaght, which adjoinable upon the Tooles, now my mortal enemies, daily oppressing my poor tenants above all others, much doubting that they be somewhat encouraged so to do, for they now being at my Lord Deputy's peace, doth no manner robbery, but upon my only tenants. His Lordship hath sundry times said he would be even with me ; but indeed, if he constrain me to lie at Tallaght, it will be odd on my behalf, for in short time I shall be in the same case with the Tooles, that my predecessor was with the Geraldine. For servants have I none, passing four

and a chaplain, which is a very slender company to
resist so many malefactors as be of the Tooles, and their
adherents at the least two hundred persons. How I am
wrapped, God judge. If I endeavour not to preach the
Word of God, then am I assured to incur my Prince's
and your Lordship's displeasure. If I repair to my
house at Tallaght, then am I assured nigh to be my
confusion. Thus am I on every side involved with
sorrows, and all I think too little if it were for my
Prince's honour."

Archbishop Browne was expelled under Queen Mary
from his See, as being a married man ; and it is thought,
adds the historian, with much simplicity, that had he not
been married he would have been also expelled, having
been a strenuous advocate for the Reformation in both
the former reigns.[1]

1547. Lease to Edward Basnet, late Dean of St.
Patrick's, Dublin, of the Rectory of Clondalkin, County
Dublin, with the tithes, &c., extending to Clondalkin,
Kilbride, Ballydonan, Nangar, Dromnaghe, &c., certain
lands in Tassagard and Conkill ; the Rectory of Esker,
in the same county ; the Rectory of Rathcowle, with the
tithes, &c. ; the Rectory of Talaught, with a messuage
and garden in the same, and the tithes, &c., in Talaught,
Newton, Oldbawne, Ballyloghan, Kylmardin, Kyltipper,
Burgholon, Glanego, Corbally, Jopeston, Kyllowan,
Whiteston, Cokeston, Prowdeston, Donyngsfelde, Bel-
garde, Newlande, Ballycarran, Newhall, Kylmanaghe,
Tymothan, Ballycullyan, Ballycrathe, and Kyllynynym,
and all the spiritual profits of said parishes to hold for

[1] See notice of George Browne in *Dictionary of National
Biography*, and *Letters and Papers of the Reign of Henry VIII*,
passim.

twenty-one years at a rent of £200; finding fit chaplains of churches of said four parishes.

The Minor Canons and Choristers of St. Patrick's had at Tallaght eight messuages, six gardens, and five and a half acres of arable land, and a custom of six hens.

1548. The Vicarage of "Tavelaghe" was given to Simon Water.

1550. A pardon was granted to George Browne, Archbishop of Dublin; William Browne, of Tawlaght; Anthony Browne, of Tawlaght; Henry Sherewood, of Tawlaght; John Raathe, Edmund Crell, Laurence Browne, and William Harrolde, of Tawlaght, for offences against certain statutes.

1573. During an invasion of the Irish into Tallaght a nephew and some servants of Adam Loftus, then Archbishop of Dublin, were slain at the gates of the palace. He writes on May 11 to the Lord Deputy urging the necessity of coercive measures, as he says the "Irishry" were never more insolent. Two years later we find Loftus entertaining the Lord Deputy as his guest at Tallaght. It was then considered the chief house of the See. One Brereton had an interest in it which Loftus was anxious to purchase, and he travelled to London on one occasion to secure the assistance of the Crown in obtaining his object.[1]

1615. The Royal Visitation of this year returns the Rectory of Tallaght as belonging to the Deanery of St. Patrick's Cathedral. Thomas Brakeshaw was the minister and preacher. The value was twenty marks; and the church and chancel were in good repair and provided with books. Whitechurch and Cruagh, which were impro-

[1] See *Irish State Papers*, and notice of Loftus in *Dictionary of National Biography*.

priate rectories, were also under the charge of the Vicar
of Tallaght. In both parishes the church and chancel
were in good repair, but unprovided with books, except
such as the clergyman brought with him. Kilnasantan,
which belonged to the economy fund of St. Patrick's,
was annexed to the vicarage of Tallaght, as was also
Templeoge. The latter parish was then in sequestration,
and the church and chancel were in ruin.[1]

1619. Launcelot Bulkeley was appointed Archbishop
of Dublin. He was ancestor of the Viscounts Bulkeley.
His son, William Bulkeley, built Old Bawn, near Tallaght. The Archbishop died at Tallaght on September 8th, 1650, in the eighty-second year of his age.

1630. Archbishop Bulkeley, in his description of his
diocese, thus mentions this parish :—"Tawlaght and
Templeoge.—The tithes of Tawlaght belong to the Dean
of St. Patrick's, Dublin. The church and chancel are in
good repair and decency. There are between three and
four score that frequent Divine Service and Sermon.
There is mass frequently said in the parish of Tawlaght,
viz., in the towns of Ballyneskorney, Ballinan, Kilnarden,
and Jobstown, sometimes in one man's house, sometimes
in another, in those towns. The tithes of Templeoge
are impropriate. Sir William Parsons, knight and baronet,
is farmer. The church is ruinous. John Hogben, clerk,

---

[1] The lands of the See at Tallaght were about this time defined
as the mountains, towns, and lands of Glasnamucky, Ballyslater,
Killnasantan, and Castle Kelly ; the mountains, towns, and lands of
Ballymakan, containing 20 acres arable, bounded on the east by
Kilbeg and Three Castles, on the south by the Common bogs, on
the west by Carrickasure, and on the north by the lands of Boyes-
town and Sheragan ; also the lands of Kiltipper, and one field on
the lands of Tallaght, on the north side of a grove on the lands of
Old Bawn, called the Cappagh Garden.

serves the cure, which is worth £5 per annum. The priests are maintained and mass frequently said in the houses of Adam Talbott of Belgart, Barnaby Rely of Timon, Mrs. Ellenore Talbott and Mrs. Henry Talbott of Templeoge, and Pierse Archbold of Knocklin, which Pierse Archbold doth maintain a Popish schoolmaster in his town. The said Hogben is Vicar of Tawlaght, which is worth £20 per annum."

1637. Richard Ellis was Vicar of Tallaght. He appears also as such in 1648. On 15th February, 1660, he was collated to the Prebend of Wicklow; in 1662 he became Prebendary of Kilrane (Ferns); and in 1667 Archdeacon and Vicar-General of Ferns. He held the Archdeaconry and Prebend of Wicklow by faculty until his death in 1683.

1638. Ordinations were held at Tallaght on May 20th, June 9th, and September 23rd. Also in 1639 on September 22nd; in 1640 on May 31st, September 20th, and December 20th; and in 1641 on June 20th and September 19th.

1657. In the *Down Survey* made in this year, "Tallaugh Parish" is thus described :—

" It is bounded on the north with the parrish of Clandalkin and Crumline; on the east and south-east with the parrish of Rafarnam and Creevagh; on the south with the barony of Talbotstowne, in the county of Wicklow ; on the west and north-west with the parrish of Castletoone and Sagard.

"The quality of the soil is good, arable, pasture, and meadow. The south of the said parish is mountainous, and grown with heath, and many places afording noe pasture.

" It contains of forfeited land those ensueing denominations, viz., Fryerstowne, Balligscorning, Temploge, Kilnarden, Jobstowne, Whitestowne, Belgardton, and Cookestowne. The improvements therein are: At Temploge there stands a castle in repair, a tuckmill, and a house out of repair; at Jobstowne, a castle in repair, and some cottages and cabbins; and at Belgard, an old castle made habitable.

		A.	R.	P.
"Mr. Luttrell, of Luttrellstowne, Fryerstowne		112	0	0
" Adam Talbott, of Belguard, Balliskorninge		180	0	0
" Same	same	657	0	0
" Sir Henry Talbott, Temploge		265	0	10
"Adam Talbott, Kilnarden		196	0	0
"Garratt Nichold, Jobstowne		229	0	0
"Adam Talbott, Whitestowne		142	0	0
" Same	Belgardstowne	222	0	0
" Same	Part of Belgardston, called Kingswood	21	3	0
" Same	Cookestowne	75	0	0
		"2,099	3	10"

1662. The Churchwardens of Tallaght exhibited a petition to the House of Lords, stating "that their church was in 1651 in good repair, with convenient pews, font, pulpit, and other necessaries, and also paved with hewn stone, all which cost the petitioners £300; that about the same time Captain Henry Alland, coming to quarter there with his troop, caused the roof of the said church to be pulled down, and converted the timber thereof for building a house to dwell in in the county of Kildare, and converted the slates of the church to his own use, and caused the paving-stones thereof to be carried to Dublin, to pave his kitchen entry and other rooms in his house, fed his horses in the font, and converted the seats and pews to his own use." The petitioners therefore prayed redress, and were decreed a sum of £100, to be levied, with all costs, off the estate of the said Captain Henry Alland.

1664. In the Hearth Money Roll of this year there appear under Tallaght : the Lord Archbishop, eight chimneys, John Jones, two chimneys, and William Brookes, two chimneys ; under Old Bawn : Mr. Archdeacon Bulkeley, twelve chimneys ; and under Templeoge : Sir Henry Talbot, five chimneys.

The Minor Canons, in this year, on the expiration of a lease to Sir James Ware, demised their lands at Tallaght to the Vicars-Choral at a rent of 30s.

1679. John Cuff collated Vicar of Tallaght. In 1681 he was appointed to Hollywood.

1685. Edward Hinde, or Hynd, was collated on 26th November to the Vicarage of Tallaght, united to Cruagh. He had been Rector of Baldungan. A sequestration of the parish, issued on 16th August, 1689, to Louis Griffith ; and in 1690 Hinde either died or resigned. He was the son of Samuel Hinde, and was born in the Isle of Man. He entered Trinity College in 1671, was elected a Scholar, graduated in 1676 B.A., and proceeded in 1679 M.A.

1690. Hugh Wilson was collated on June 4th to the Vicarage of Tallaght, united to Clondalkin ; Whitechurch and Cruagh having been severed from Tallaght and united to the Archdeaconry of Dublin. He entered Trinity College as a sizar, aged 18, on 8th June, 1680, and was ordained, being B.A., priest in Christ Church Cathedral on Trinity Sunday, 22nd May, 1688, by William [Moreton], Bishop of Kildare. On 4th May of same year he was licensed as " reader " in St. Nicholas Without. On 24th May, 1699, he was collated to Whitechurch and Cruagh, which were again united to

Tallaght ; and on 19th November, 1701, he was appointed
Prebendary of Kilmactalway in St. Patrick's Cathedral.
We find him on 15th April, 1696, at the induction of
Henry Rocheblave to the Vicarage of Dunlavan ; and
again, on 6th April, 1703, present at the election of
Proctors to Convocation for the Dublin Diocese.   On
2nd February, 1727, he was collated Prebendary of
Swords, and died in 1735.

1701. Fletewood Fisher appointed on 2nd December
to Vicarage Cruagh, alias Crevagh.

1706. Mr. Jones licensed on 27th February as schoolmaster at Tallaght.

1707. John Griffith licensed on 24th July as schoolmaster of Cruagh and Kilgobbin.

1708. William King, then Archbishop of Dublin,
writes, on September 7th in this year, to the Bishop of
Down (Edward Smyth, who had been previously Dean
of St. Patrick's) :—" I am very thankful to you for your
promise to contribute to repair the church of Tallaght.[1]
Bp. Lindsay [Bishop of Killaloe, who had also been
previously Dean of St. Patrick's] gives 15*l*., which we
have, to your 15*l*. more, will enable us to go on with
the work.   There is a great inclination, God be thanked,
in people to repair churches.   Twelve have been built
since I was Archbishop in this diocese, or paid for ; six
or seven are going on ; and yet I shall want ten or twelve
more."[2]

---

[1] A return of this date says :—" There are two churches in repair
—one at Tallaugh, another at Clondalkin—served alternately; there
wants a third at Whitechurch.   There were anciently several churches
and chapels in this parish ; but are, most of them, extinct or lost."

[2] Correspondence of Archbishop King, in Library of Trinity
College, Dublin.

1727. Zachary Norton was collated on 23rd March to vicarage of Tallaght and curacy of Whitechurch, on resignation of Mr. Hugh Wilson. He was the son of William Norton, and was born in the Co. Wexford. On 17th May, 1703, he entered Trinity College as a sizar, at the age of twenty, having been educated in Dublin under Dr. Jones. He was elected a scholar in 1707, graduated B.A. in 1708, and proceeded M.A. in 1712. On 7th November, 1730, he was appointed to the Prebend of Donaghmore, and resigned Tallaght and Whitechurch.

The first vestry books extant in the parish date from this time. They are filled with reports of the Vestry meetings held for the appointment of parish officers. The Vestry also struck rates on the acreage of Tallaght, Whitechurch, and Cruagh, for the repairs of the church, and suchlike purposes. Vestries were also held for badging paupers, who were thereby licensed to beg; while unbadged beggars were liable to imprisonment.[1] There was a parish officer, generally known by the name of " Bang-beggar," whose duty it was to see that none but licensed beggars should exercise this calling ; and the father of a late bishop held the honourable post of " Bang-beggar " for the town of New Ross.

1729. Archbishop John Hoadly pulled down a great part of the old Castle of Tallaght. It appears to have been a very extensive pile, on the site of the ancient monastic edifice, which existed until 1324, when Archbishop de Bicknor rebuilt it. Archbishop Hoadly

---

[1] Some of the badges issued to beggars are to be seen in the Museum of the Royal Irish Academy, now in the National Museum. " Badged beggars " are similar to the " Blue Gowns " mentioned in Sir Walter Scott's *Antiquary*.

with the materials built a mansion which Austin Cooper
in 1779 thus describes:—" The archiepiscopal palace of
the See of Dublin, for a thing of its kind, is the poorest
I ever saw.   It is a large piece of patchwork, so void
of either order or regularity that it is past describing.
Adjoining it is a long range of stables, &c., at the end
of which is a square castle.   What to call it I am at a
loss.   I should imagine it to be a part of the old
monastery that formerly stood here.   It commands more
antiquity in its appearance than the palace, as it has
some of the Gothic taste in it, which I could not see in
the other.   I went into a coach-house adjoining this, and
saw in it a very large arch, stopped up, so that some
other building joined.   Archbishop Hoadly was the last
man who resided in it, and the modern repairs in it were
done by him.   When I again visited this place (1780), I
found it bear a much more agreeable aspect.   All the
patchwork of brick and stone is destroyed by an universal dashing and whitewashing, new windows, and the
crevices of the old stone-work filled with mortar.   All
this thorough repairing was done last summer (I sup-
pose) by his worthy Grace the present Archbishop."
This is rather negative praise.   A further description
of the palace will be found later on.

Archbishop Hoadly was a great agriculturist.   His
daughter, and only child, who married Bellingham Boyle,
had similar tastes ; and, in an amusing letter, Swift thanks
her for a pig and some butter which she had sent him
from Tallaght.   She was a favourite of the Dean ; he
commends her love of housewifery and good sense, and
writes on one occasion in great distress on hearing
she was ill with the smallpox.   Hoadly resigned the
See of Dublin in 1742, on being appointed to the

Primacy. He died in 1746, and was buried at Tallaght with his wife, who had died two years previously.

1730. John Gill collated on 20th November to the vicarage of Tallaght and Rectory of Cruagh, and licensed as Curate of Whitechurch. He was born in Dublin, and entered Trinity College on 6th April, 1714, aged sixteen, having been educated in Dublin under Dr. Wallace. He graduated B.A., 1719, and proceeded M.A., 1722. On 9th April, 1731, he was collated to the Rectory of Castlemacadam, and resigned Tallaght.

1731. Zachary Norton collated on 10th April for the second time to Tallaght, which he held until 6th June, 1737, when he was appointed Precentor of Ferns. He resigned in 1760, and died, "aged upwards of ninety," in March, 1767.

1732. Tallaght, Whitechurch, and Cruagh were united by Act of Privy Council on 23rd June, the consent of Zachary Norton, incumbent, of the Rev. John Wynne, patron, of the Rev. Robert Spence, in remainder, and of the Archbishop of Dublin, having been obtained. This Act was not enrolled, as ordered ; and on 23rd September, 1734, another Act was made to the same effect, signed by "John Dublin, Granard, Molesworth, Ar : Meath, John Rogerson, Tho : Marlay, Tho : Taylor, Edwd. Webster, W. Graham."

1734. Sir Compton Domvile, of Templeogue, and the Right Hon. James Tynte, of Old Bawn, were appointed overseers and directors of roads.

1737. Robert Trotter collated on 13th June to vicarage of Tallaght. He was son of John Trotter, gentleman ; and was born near Enniskillen. Having been educated in the County Tyrone under Master Ballantine, he entered Trinity College on 9th May, 1722, and graduated B.A. in 1727. On 9th July, 1737, he was appointed to the Prebend of Timolhan, and died in December following.

1738. John Gill was on 7th February again instituted to vicarage of Tallaght, presented by Rev. John Wynne ; as Norton had done, so likewise did he.

1740. John Jones collated on 1st June to Tallaght, on the death of John Gill. He was a son of Captain William Jones, and was born in the County Kilkenny. He entered Trinity College on 8th March, 1735, when nineteen years of age, was elected a scholar, graduated B.A. in 1739, and proceeded M.A. and LL.D. In *The Dublin Gazette* for 29th July, 1740, it is announced that "last Wednesday the Rev. Mr. Jones, Minister of Tallow, near this city, was married to Miss Downes, a gentlewoman of great parts and fortune." He expended in 1743 £52 14s. 8d. on improvements at the glebe, and £2 5s. 6d. on making a buffet in the parlour. He resigned in 1743.

1742. Charles Cobbe[1] was Archbishop; he purchased large tracts of Church lands in Tallaght Parish, and, bequeathing them to his relatives, died in 1765.

1743. Owen Sheill instituted on 21st March to Tallaght on the presentation of Rev. John Wynne. He was probably son of Owen Sheill, master of the Diocesan School, who was buried at St. Patrick's in 1743. In 1737 he was licensed, 5th November, to the mastership of the Free School of St. Patrick's, and on October 8th to the curacy of St. Luke's. In 1748 he was admitted M.A. in Dublin University. He died in 1769.

---

[1] See notice of him in *Dictionary of National Biography*.

1744. A subscription was made amongst the parishioners to put a coved ceiling in the church, and to do other needful repairs. The two bells were then re-hung.[1]

1766. Arthur Smyth[2] was Archbishop. He bequeathed £50 for the use of the poor of Tallaght. He died in 1771.

1769. Oliver Turkington nominated on 20th November parish clerk of Tallaght by Owen Sheill, M.A., Vicar.

1769. John Elton was collated to Tallaght on the death of Owen Sheill. He was son of Anthony Elton, and was born in the County Wicklow. He entered Trinity College on 11th May, 1737, and graduated B.A. 1742, subsequently proceeding M.A. He died in 1783.

1770. James Robinson nominated, on 24th May, 1770, schoolmaster of Tallaght, on nomination of John Elton.

1771. "Ye Paten or Salver bought at ye cost of ye Parish."

1774. At a Vestry held on 13th September this year, it was resolved "that the bell given in exchange by Mr. Goodison for the two cracked bells of the parish is not so good as either of them in sound and clearness, and that the churchwardens do apply forthwith for a better bell."

1775. Mark Wainwright was nominated on December 5th curate of Tallaght, by John Elton, at £50 per annum. He was appointed on 21st April, 1780, Rector of Cloghran by the Crown.

---

[1] In the Register of the Diocese of Dublin, the yearly value or Tallaght, in the year 1744, is given as £110.

[2] See notice of him in *Dictionary of National Biography*.

1778. In *The Freeman's Journal* of February 19-21, the following appears :—

> "A Card. The parishioners of T-ll-w present their respects to the R-v-d D-c-r E-lt-n, and inform him that they are unanimously determined to petition the A-hb-p unless he immediately appoints a curate to officiate in said parish, or pays a more regular attendance himself; the congregation only consisting of a few, or a fracture in a single pane of glass, is but a shallow excuse for non-attendance for five weeks past. If this hint should not have the desired effect, the D-r may expect a more minute description to be laid before the public."

1778. Robert Fowler,[1] Archbishop of Dublin, expended £3,582 12s. 4d. in buildings and repairs at Tallaght, and at St. Sepulchre's in Dublin, and soon after expended a further sum of £1,397 18s. 8d. He enclosed the large garden behind the palace with a good wall still standing. Some say he altered the course of the road to its present line, as it ran formerly from the old turnpike across to the Greenhills Road, leaving the palace on the right-hand side. Being fond of agricultural pursuits, he levelled several ditches, and made many other improvements. He built also a bath-house, in the wall of which he utilized part of the old Cross of Tallaght, which had stood from time immemorial in the middle of the town. He died in 1801.

1781. Rev. David Wilson was curate.

1782. Samuel Hodson was nominated on 13th May curate of Tallaght, by John Elton, at £50 per annum.

1782. Ann Murray was paid on 2nd April £2 for acting as pound-keeper during the year. The parishioners agreed to support expense of prosecutions against

---

[1] See notice of him in *Dictionary of National Biography*.

any person or persons who might break into the pound to rescue their cattle.

1783. At a Vestry it was proposed that a throne be erected, or a suitable pew enclosed, for the use of His Grace the Archbishop, in Tallaght Church. Archbishop Fowler declined the honour, as he said that one seat should not be more decorated than another in a parish church.

1783. Sequestration on September 1st of Vicarage of Tallaght and Curacy of Whitechurch, &c., to Rev. John Drury.

1784. The Rev. Samuel Hodson, curate, was grievously assaulted when leaving the vestry-room, by a daughter of John Maxwell, the parish clerk. She insulted and abused his reverence to such a degree that the whole parish was moved with indignation. A Vestry was held forthwith, at which a memorial was prepared to the Archbishop, praying His Grace to remove the said John Maxwell from his clerkship, as he had made himself so obnoxious as to prevent memorialists from attending church; and stating that he had invented and propagated a false, scandalous, and malicious accusation against the Rev. Samuel Hodson, tending to lessen his good name and character; and that the said John Maxwell, in order to keep up the spirit of his false and malicious accusation, and with malevolent design, had frequently selected from the Divine Psalms such passages as would tend to answer his malevolent purpose, and to traduce by implication the character of the said Samuel Hodson, and had sung such parts of the Psalms during the Divine Service. At a subsequent Vestry held on 12th April, 1784, it was agreed to present a piece of plate value £5, with a suitable address, to the Rev. S.

Hodson, as a small tribute of esteem and as a token of condolence under his grievances.

1784. William Bryan, B.A., was presented on 15th February to Tallaght, by his uncle, William Bryan, of the City of Dublin, merchant. He resigned on 5th June, 1790, and was appointed on the 15th to the Rectory of Kilcronaghan, in the Diocese of Derry; with which he held the benefice of Kilkenny West, in the Diocese of Meath, by faculty dated 8th July, 1809. He died 13th March, 1817, and was buried at Desertmartin old church-yard in the same grave with his father, the Rev. Robert Bryan, who died on 16th March, 1776, aged sixty-six years.

1786. Commission on Tallaght Glebe House appointed on 19th June on petition of Catherine Elton, widow of John Elton.

1787. Commission appointed on 12th July to view improvements for Rev. William Bryan. Cost found to be £110 9s. 10d.

1790. The parishioners presented Rev. William Bryan with a piece of plate, value £10, as a small tribute of their esteem and appreciation of his conduct as a minister of the Gospel, and also as a spirited, active, and fearless magistrate in those stirring times.

Anthony Armstrong appointed clerk, which post he held for nearly fifty years.

1790. Robert Cochrane was collated on June 11th to the vicarage of Tallaght, Curacy of Whitechurch, and Rectory of Cruagh, by the Archbishop, to whom Mr. William Bryan had given the presentation.

1790. Grant from Archbishop on 4th June of two acres for a school in Tallaght.

1792. "A Vestry was held in the parish church of

Tallaght, which was very numerously attended, the minister in the chair, at which a motion was made and carried, with only two dissentients, to levy a tax of one penny per acre on the lands in that parish, to be appropriated towards rebuilding the Roman Catholic chapel in that district."

1795. It was agreed, at a Vestry Meeting on 13th November, that £69 16s. was to be levied off the parish of Tallaght to pay eleven men to serve as substitutes in the County Dublin Militia.

1797. Matthew Handcock, of Fir House, appointed churchwarden.

1799. Payment of 1s. 1d. was ordered for making a grave for a robber who was murdered in the mountains.

1806. A new vestry-room was built on the north side of the church, adjoining the minister's garden.

1807. At a Vestry it was ordered that the churchwardens should carry the poor box through the church on Sundays, or forfeit 1s. 1d. for each time of default.

1807. In the Ecclesiastical Report of this year the parishes are thus described :—" Tallaght, a curacy ; Whitechurch, do. ; Cruagh, *alias* Crevagh, a rectory, all contiguous ; extent, from east to west, five miles ; from north to south, five miles. Incumbent, Robert Cochrane, literate, has cure of souls ; resident in the glebe house, and discharges the duties ; the benefices perpetually united, time not known. One church in good repair in the parish of Tallaght, a glebe house in same, and 16 acres of glebe contiguous to the church. No curate."

1809. Paid for the carriage of the Ten Commandments home, 2s. 8d.

1810. A wall ordered to be built round part of the churchyard.

1813. Rev. Thomas Goff appointed Vicar. This was probably Mr. Goff of Oak Park, Co. Roscommon, who died in October, 1844.

June 6th. Lundy Foot, churchwarden, bought from John Bennet one large bell, weighing 9 cwts. 3 qrs. 4 lb., at 2s. 6d. per lb., £137. There was received for the old bell, weighing 1 cwt. 3 qrs. 19 lb., at 1s. 1d. per lb., £10 15s.; and Mr. Blackburne was paid for hanging the same, £68 6s.

1815. Rev. Thomas Strong, Curate.

1820. Rev. J. Groves, Curate.

1821. Rev. J. C. M'Causland, Curate. He was the last person who lived in the old palace, which shortly after was pulled down. The Rev. Mr. Lovett succeeded him as Curate. He was tutor to Isaac Butt, who afterwards became rather notorious, and who, when a lad, used to drive four goats and a little phaeton about the country.

1821. An Act of Parliament, 1 & 2 Geo. IV, cap. 15, 28th May, 1821, was passed at the instance of Archbishop Beresford, divesting the Archbishop of Dublin of Tallaght as a palace, and placing the mensal lands attached to it in the same circumstances as other See lands. The Act states that the buildings and offices on this demesne were then in such a state of decay as to be unfit for habitation; that a country residence for the Archbishop was unnecessary, and that the income of the See was inadequate to support the expense of two establishments; the Archbishop was, therefore, empowered to demise the same for the usual term. The following is the schedule annexed to the said Act:—

				A.	R.	P.
The palace, offices, yard, and hay-yard			...	0	3	28
Castle garden ...	...	...	...	0	2	0
Melon yard ...	...	...	...	0	2	2
Large garden ...	...	...	...	4	1	34
Front lawn and pond ...	...	...	0	2	25
Large lawn and pond ...	...	...	1	0	0
Field in possession of Kelly	...	...	1	0	17
Arable meadows and pasture	...	...	17	0	20
Garden and orchard ...	...	...	1	2	20
Glebe ...	...	...	...	0	2	0
Demesne ...	...	...	...	174	1	23

Plantation measure, 202   2 29

1822. William Trocke, M.A., Dub., appointed Vicar.

1822. Archbishop Magee sold the demesne to Major Palmer, then Inspector-General of Prisons, who undertook to demolish the old palace, lest it should ever become a monastic institution. Major Palmer accordingly pulled it all down, and occupied, it is said, two years in removing the materials. With part of them he built a fine mansion-house. He built also the school-house, and several cottages in the town, and repaired the roads in the neighbourhood. Nothing remained of the old palace but a great vault, formerly part of the kitchen, now a mound covered with trees. Major Palmer disposed of his interest at Tallaght to Mr. Lentaigne.[1] The latter kept the great gardens, enclosed by Archbishop Fowler, in good order, and made further improvements. In 1842 he leased the greater portion of the demesne to the Dominicans, who have built the present monastery, on the site of the old Castle, as hereafter mentioned.

[1] Afterwards the Right Hon. Sir John Lentaigne.

1830. William Robinson, M.A., Dub., appointed Vicar. He held the union of Tallaght, Whitechurch, and Cruagh for fifty-seven years, and resigned in 1887. His death (*ætatis* eighty-four) took place at Tallaght Glebe House on 9th November of the same year, and his interment in the parish churchyard on the Saturday following. Mr. Robinson was ordained in 1827.[1]

1869. William Elias Handcock elected on 7th September lay representative of the parish, in pursuance of a circular issued by His Grace the Archbishop of Dublin.

1871. The Select Vestry unanimously decided, on 22nd September, to object to the severance of the long-established union of the parishes of Tallaght, Cruagh, and Whitechurch.

1880. The Select Vestry decided on 19th July to oppose the severance of Cruagh from Tallaght union.

1882. On October 1st the foundation-stone of the new Dominican Church, St. Mary of the Rosary, was solemnly blessed and laid by the Cardinal Archbishop of Dublin. The church is of the early English style, and measures 140 feet in length. A beautiful rood-screen divides the building into equal portions, one of which is occupied by the sanctuary and choir.

The remains of the celebrated preacher, Dr. Burke, are laid in one of the side chapels. A large new wing is now being added, which will connect the church and convent.

1887. Eugene Henry O'Meara, M.A., elected Vicar of Tallaght, and is the present Incumbent. He was previously Rector of Newcastle Lyons.

[1] In the Parliamentary Returns of 1864 the net value of this vicarage is given as £206 5s. 4d.

TALLAGHT CASTLE AND TOWN.

N 1310 the bailiffs of Tamelag, or Tallaght, had a royal grant in aid of enclosing their town. In 1324 Archbishop Alexander de Bicknor built the Castle of Tallaght, on the site of the monastery that had existed there from St. Maelruain's time. The altered state of affairs rendered it necessary to fortify such places, and this castle was frequently enlarged and altered during the disturbed and troubled years, that may be called the Dark Ages of Ireland—from 1300 to 1600. The frontispiece to this book, if a correct view, will give an idea of the stately edifice that once stood in the little village of Tallaght. It was probably in the form of a square, with a large court or bawn in the centre, surrounded by lofty buildings and walls. The many foundations that have been from time to time uncovered show how extensive these must have been. I have not been able to trace from what sketch this view was engraved, but have heard that in the salon of the old palace there were painted medallions on the walls, representing the different progressive stages of the castle and buildings. It may have been from some of these that the sketch was taken. The plate is now very rare.[1]

[1] Sir William Wilde says that this engraving was made in 1818, and was intended for Mason's projected History of Christ Church Cathedral. (See *Journal of the R. H. and A. A. of Ireland*, vol. i, Pt. I, p. 39.) The proof engraving is in the Monastery of Tallaght. It is dedicated to His Grace Euseby [Cleaver], Archbishop of Dublin, by W. Monck Mason, and bears the date January 1st, 1818.

In 1332, O'Toole of Imaile, at the head of a numerous train of armed followers, plundered the Palace of Tallaght, carried away a prey of three hundred sheep, slew many of the Archbishop's servants, and defeated, in a pitched battle, Sir Philip Brett and a body of the citizens of Dublin, who came against him. Watch and ward were afterwards constantly kept here, and at Bray, to repel similar attacks.

In 1356, Walter Russell, being Constable of Tallaght Castle, the Lord Lieutenant entered into a compact with one of the O'Tooles, whereby the latter, with forty hobillers, or horsemen, and forty armed foot, was to defend the English marches, from Tallaght to Windgates, against the invasions of his countrymen. In the following year, the said Walter Russell was directed to levy from the vicinage reasonable pledges and subsidies for maintaining the wards stationed on these marches.

In 1378, Matthew, the son of Redmond de Bermingham, took his station here, with 120 hobillers, to resist the O'Byrnes; and, in the same year, John de Wade received £20 from the King's Exchequer, as a remuneration for two horses, and other goods of his, burned at Tallaght by the O'Nolans.

In 1448, by an Act of Parliament of that date, Tallaght, with other towns, was privileged to take custom.

In 1540, the O'Tooles invaded and devastated this and the adjacent Royal Manors, with deadly enmity and destruction.[1]

---

[1] In the reign of Henry VIII the O'Tooles were only restrained by armed force. Lord Deputy Skeffington writes, in 1535, that

In 1729, Archbishop Hoadly demolished the castle, using the materials to build the palace, as previously mentioned ; and the Archbishops of Dublin used it until 1821 as a country residence.[1]

Brewer, in his *Beauties of Ireland*, describes the palace as a spacious, but long and narrow, building, composed of the grey stone of the country, and destitute of pretensions to architectural beauty. He says : " The interior contains many apartments of ample proportions, but none that are highly embellished. The hall, into which the visitor is conducted by a flight of stone steps, measures twenty-one feet square, and is lighted by two tiers of windows. The dining-room is twenty-five feet in length, by twenty-one in width, and is ornamented with the archiepiscopal arms, impaled with a shield, quarterly, charged in the first quarter with a pigeon. The date is 1729, and, above, is the crest, a hawk perched on a round ball. Underneath the coat of arms

portion of his forces lie at Tallaght. Two years later Robert Cowley, a well-known official, writes to Lord Cromwell that Ballymore and Tallaght are the most important places for the defence of the counties of Dublin and of Kildare against the O'Tooles and the O'Byrnes, and that tenants should be placed there, who would prove " hardy warders," able to defend the Pale.—*State Papers of Henry VIII.*

[1] Gabriel Beranger made a sketch of the palace in 1771. Some of it was apparently dilapidated. He says : " The right wing is modern, and the steps still more, being new and being made of cut mountain stone." Of the tower he says : " It seems to have been a gate of a much larger building of which this tower only remains. The arch is half stopped up and mended with brick. I was told it was intended to make a summer-house of it."—Wilde's *Memoir of Gabriel Beranger.*

is the following inscription :—" Johannes Hoadly, hanc
domum refecit."[1] The great drawing-room, or salon,
measures thirty-three feet by twenty-one, and contains
the only portrait in the palace—a full-length of Archbishop Hoadly, who was translated to the See of Dublin
in January, 1729. The library is a small apartment,
having a window of large dimensions, from which, as
from all the windows of the reception-rooms, very fine
views are obtained of Montpellier Hill, and the adjacent tract of captivating scenery. The gardens are
disposed with unpleasing formality, but the antiquary
will derive some gratification from finding here the
remains of a tower, which constituted an integral part of
the former palace. Archbishop Fowler, translated to
Dublin in 1773, surrounded the demesne with a wall,
and bestowed other improvements."

One small tower, part of the old castle, was left
standing, and still remains, though much altered. The

---

[1] The coat of arms and inscription were on the chimney-piece.
This chimney-piece is now in Tubrid Church, in the Diocese of
Lismore, where it was brought by the Rev. Henry Palmer, brother
of Major Palmer, who was then Rector of that Parish. His son, also
the Rev. Henry Palmer, in a letter to the Rev. C. T. M'Cready, D.D.,
dated 21st October, 1885, says: "I perfectly remember, when
quite a boy, some sixty years ago, being taken up to Tallaght by
my father to the handsome modern mansion, which my uncle,
Major Palmer, Inspector-General of Prisons, built, having pulled
down the fine old palace. . . . My dear father saved, as *spolia
opima* out of the ruins, the noble chimney-piece in question, and
went to the expense of having it brought by sea to Waterford, and
thence here, and erecting it in his church. I remember a mitre
came with it ; but it was not thought becoming to have it replaced
on the summit of the apex after having fallen from its high
estate !" (Information kindly given by Dr. M'Cready.)

accompanying sketch represents it in 1770.   It was
repaired in 1835 [1] by Mr. Lentaigne, who then had in it

TALLAGHT CASTLE.

a great collection of curiosities, including a small brass
coin found at Tallaght, having on one side an ecclesiastic
holding a long staff, thus ·ȷ·, with a Latin inscription
round the margin, and on the reverse, "IVO" in two or

---

[1] In the same year, close to the site of the Palace, a bulla of Pope
Leo X was discovered when a field was being ploughed.   Sir John
Lentaigne presented it to the Dominican Fathers, in whose possession it now is.   The bulla is of lead, and about the size of the
large penny of George IV.   On one side is the inscription in large
Damascene letters " Leo Papa X."   On the reverse are two vesica-
shaped panels ; in one of these is the traditional head of St. Peter,
and in the other that of St. Paul.   Between these panels is a Latin
cross, over which are the letters " S.S. PE. PA."   There is no date,
but it is in a state of perfect preservation.   The bulla was attached
by a silk or parchment band to the Papal Bulls, and served as a seal
to guarantee the authenticity of the document.

three places; and a round stone, four inches in diameter, gradually sloping from the centre to the edge, which was found there, and which was probably one of those blessed stones which are still remembered and revered in different parts of Ireland. In repairing the staircase, Mr. Lentaigne found a head carved in stone, which was firmly set in the wall, with the back part outwards. This fact shows that the builders made use of the materials of the ancient church or monastery which had stood there centuries before. The head is not of ordinary size, the nose is partially broken off, the chin low and retreating, the eyes prominent, and placed high up, with a very low forehead; the face is rather long, and the workmanship is rude. There was a long house, which is now the chapel, attached to the castle. Formerly part of it was used as a brewery, and the adjacent field was known as the hop garden, which proves that the archbishops brewed their own beer. Subsequently it was used as a granary and stables. It apparently was of the same age as the castle.

The archbishop's palace has been now completely removed, excepting, as before stated, one large and strong vault, over which the archbishop's dining-room was placed. This vault is now completely overgrown with trees, planted either by Major Palmer or Mr. Lentaigne. There is a fine raised walk within the garden, running from north to south, called the "Friars' Walk," with a round, moat-like eminence at the north end, called the "Bishop's Seat." This walk was planted on each side with large elm and yew trees, the best of which were recently cut down. To the right of the walk stands an immense walnut tree of great age, called "St. Maelruain's Tree." It looks like two trees arising from one stem; but it was originally one stem of about

ten feet high, dividing into two branches, which towards
the end of the last century separated about five feet from
the ground. It still remains healthy, and bears loads of
fruit. Many of the branches rest on the ground, and,
having taken root, serve to prop the tree. It is a wonderful tree, and must be many hundred years old.[1] When
a bath-house which had been built by Archbishop Fowler
was being cleared by Mr. Lentaigne, the workmen found
at the bottom a round lump of granite. It has a hole
through the middle, remarkable for being cut in a screw
form, which looks as if the pedestal of a cross had been
screwed into it. This stone is now lying at the end of
the " Friars' Walk ;" and there are also lying, about
half-way up the walk, some fragments of the old cross of
Tallaght, referred to under the year 1778. In clearing
out part of the fosse, which was said originally to have
surrounded the castle, the workmen turned up another
shapeless mass of stone, about 200 pounds weight, with
a round cavity, about one foot deep, and one foot wide
at the top, tapering to the bottom. It must have been
one of the old holy water fonts ; in workmanship it cor-
responds with the other stone and the font in the churchyard, all these being certainly older than the monastery.
This stone is said to be foreign porphyry, and may have
had a history in bygone times, like the celebrated Liafail,
or stone of destiny. The moat was of great depth, and
was supplied from the Jobstown stream, about a mile
from Tallaght, from whence it was brought in an ancient
watercourse.[2]

[1] A picture of this tree will be found in O'Hanlon's *Lives of the
Irish Saints*, vol. i, frontispiece.

[2] In a note left by Mr. Handcock it is related that when Archbishop Hoadly was enclosing this stream, he attempted to build up

The foregoing account was written about forty years ago, by Eugene O'Curry : since then there have been many changes.   Mr. Lentaigne leased the principal part of the old manor of Tallaght to the Dominican Friars, who, as before stated, have built a large monastery there. In the garden lies the disjointed skeleton of an immense whale, taken on the coast of Mayo, about 1840, and brought here by Mr. Lentaigne at great expense.   He made a lofty arch in the garden with the vertebrae strung on iron bars, the ends of which were embedded in two great millstones about four feet in diameter, and two feet thick, with large square holes for the axles.   He brought these from the old powder-mills at Corkagh, near Clondalkin, where they had been used for crushing the powder until, in 1787, the mills were blown up.[1]

some steps, but was compelled to desist by a man who proved a Cromwellian title to the ground.   It appeared that he was the descendant of one Grumbly, a blacksmith in Tallaght in Cromwell's time, who had bought the field from one of the Parliament soldiers for 5s. and a griddle of cakes that happened to be baking on his hearth at the time, and who had taken care to duly register the purchase.

[1] At the right-hand side of the road coming from Dublin stands a small square tower, attached to some cottages, known locally as "Bancroft's Castle."   Mr. Dix thinks the name is derived from Irish words meaning the "Bawn of the Cattle Stealers."—See *Irish Builder* for October 15th, 1898.

THE CHURCH OF TALLAGHT.

THE present Church of Tallaght stands about eight yards from the site of a former one, and parallel to it, though much larger. It was built in 1829, by a grant from the Board of First Fruits, and was partially constructed with the materials of the old church. It is a handsome Gothic edifice, with seven lancet windows at each side, and three at each end. The walls are faced with limestone, and there are pinnacles very neatly cut all round the roof. The entrance is through a small porch, which joins the church to the old belfry, an Anglo-Norman building. The belfry is of considerable height, with three floors, to which access is gained by a winding stone staircase in the solid wall. The top is castellated, and there are three openings for bells. At least two small bells hung in these until 1774. There appears a notice in the vestry-book of that year that two cracked bells were exchanged for one large one. This was hung in the centre of the tower; but, as it did not turn out well, a new bell was bought, as before mentioned, in June, 1813, at a cost of £137. It has, too, become cracked, and does not give a full sound.[1]

The entrance to the former church was through this tower. The church comprised a centre aisle, with large

---

[1] In 1892 this bell was recast at a cost of £46. It bears the names of the incumbent, Rev. E. H. O'Meara, and of the then churchwardens, J. Neill and T. Bryan.

square pews on either side; and the pulpit, surmounted
by a sounding-board, was placed half-way down on the
right hand. The aisle was flagged with large tomb-
stones, some of which are still to be seen not far from
the gateway of the churchyard. The one belonging to Sir
John Talbot is said to have lain at the foot of the Altar
or Communion Table. At the end of the church were
the Ten Commandments, painted on a panel, which
was taken away at the time the old church was pulled
down, and no one knows what became of it.

D'Alton relates, in his *History of the County Dublin*,
that the old church was covered with memorials of archbishops and parishioners, and that, on removing one of
the pews, a chalice of glass and some human skulls were
discovered. From those who remember the building, I
can hear no confirmation of this statement. The only
monument was one to Sir Timothy Allen, which is now
in the present church, and there was also a marble slab
near the door, which recorded that this Sir Timothy
Allen had greatly improved the church.

When the old church was being removed, the workmen found a leaden coffin, containing, it is said, the
remains of Archbishop Hoadly's lady. One of them
cut the leaden coffin into strips. These he rolled round
his body, and, walking into Dublin, sold the metal.
This rather sacrilegious act was not known for some
time after.

Beneath the foundations of the old church were found
the foundations of a still older edifice, built in rude
style, with round, uncut stones, probably one of the
chapels or anchorite cells which abounded in Ireland
after the introduction of Christianity.

The church and tower stand in the centre of a raised

earth-work, and most of the churchyard is surrounded
by a lofty mound, which formerly had a deep fosse on
the outside, now filled up. To the east of the tower,
and about forty yards from it, lies neglected on the
ground a most curious ancient font of a horseshoe form.
It is five and a half feet long, by five feet six inches
deep, is very rudely made, and apparently of great
antiquity. It is cracked at one side, but could easily
be made to hold water. This is probably the identical
font out of which Captain Alland fed his horses. The
country people call it St. Moll Rooney's Lossit.[1]

There were several stone crosses of rude workmanship in the churchyard; but the only remains of these
is the base of one, with the stump of a cross in the
centre of it. It was called St. Moll Rooney's griddle
and loaf. So much for tradition, for this female saint
meant no other than the celebrated St. Maelruain, whose
festival, or patron, or pattern, was celebrated each year
on the 7th of July, and thus continued uninterruptedly
from the year 792 down to 1874. It had then so de-
generated that it became a mere excuse for drunkenness
and debauchery, and was put an end to by the monks
of Tallaght Monastery, now called St. Mary's of the
Rosary.

The custom on these occasions was to make an effigy,
supposed to represent the patron saint, and carry it
about in procession. Of late years the country people
assembled from all parts, and many came from Dublin
to be present. A favourite fiddler or piper, or some

[1] In 1890 it was placed on granite blocks in front of the church.
Underneath it there is a large vault built of brick. Many similar
vaults extended under the ancient church, and on their being
opened a few years ago, a number of skeletons were found in them.

such musician, headed the procession, which went from house to house in the village, stopping before each door until the occupants came out and danced either a jig or a reel, or both, to the music. After the procession had made its progress, a collection was made, the proceeds of which were spent in drinking. Almost every house was converted into a beer-shop for the occasion ; and the remainder of the night was spent in dancing, drinking, and fighting.

For many years it was the custom to comply with the dying request of an old piper named Burley O'Toole, who for many years performed at the pattern, to visit his grave, where the people used to dance and fight after their manner. This grew to be so disgraceful, that it was entirely put a stop to in July, 1873, by the influence of Father Purcell, of Tallaght.[1]

The old stone font was visited on these occasions. It is traditionally stated that this was used in early times for the purpose of washing the feet of the pilgrims who frequented the sacred shrines at Tallaght. The blessed well which supplied the water was only large enough to dip one can into, and was situated near the font. In later times a glebe-house was built close to the church, and this well was then covered over, and was utilized to supply water to the house by means of a pump erected in the kitchen.

---

[1] There was a man living at Tallaght in former times who was known as " the prophecy man." Amongst other things, he said that churchyards would refuse to admit dead bodies ; that there would be a camp on the Curragh of Kildare ; that poorhouses would be built ; that France and Spain would get up a dance, and England pay the piper ; and that the Pope would be upset and Rome plundered.—Note left by Mr. Handcock.

In 1791 Mr. Cochrane, then the Vicar, had an auction. Many of the old people who remembered the well took the opportunity of getting a drink of its miraculous waters. The glebe-house has long since disappeared; and though the well now is covered up, it could easily be found by its proximity to the font. Indeed, it may have been this well which was found by the present Incumbent. He had a large heap of manure in the field, and one day observed a great hole in the centre of the heap, and on investigation found that it was the roof of an old well that had fallen in. It is now filled up, but a slight depression marks the spot. Another tradition is that there were in old times two chapels in Tallaght—one for the parish, and one for the friary. These were connected by an underground passage, through which the clergy always passed in going from one chapel to the other, and never were seen by the people except at Mass. When they officiated, they came up steps behind the altar with lighted candles in their hands, thus astonishing the natives, who might have imagined that they were rising from the lower regions. This passage is still talked of, and within living men's memory it is said that it was opened, and that a man went some way into it, and found an old sword, so decayed that it fell to pieces in his hand.

The interior of the present church is lofty, the roof apparently supported by six great Gothic arches. There are seats for about 200. The building is damp and cold.[1] There are monuments in it to Sir Timothy Allen, as before mentioned, to Matthew Handcock, to Rev. T. Ryan, to Mrs. Clancy, and to J. Robinson.[2] The

---

[1] See Appendix B.   [2] See Appendix C.

attendance of the parishioners averages seventy-five.
There are no pew-rents ; but the principal houses in the
parish have special pews allotted to them. The churchyard, which is very extensive, contains half an acre.
The graves are laid east and west, with the head-stones
facing the east.

In old times the road from Blessington ran from the
corner near the church, where the turnpike stood, across
to the Greenhills Road, leaving the castle on the right
hand. Either Archbishop Hoadly or Archbishop Fowler
may have altered it to the present line. There was an
ancient smith's forge nearly opposite the church, on the
side of the old road. The cinders were to be seen on
raising the sods. The corner between the Belgard and
Tallaght Road was called the Dean's Acre, and is
mentioned in old ecclesiastical writings. There were
only two houses of any note in Tallaght. One of them,
at the church end of the town, was called " the mitre
house," from the gables being mitred. It is now inhabited by Mr. Doyle, and is nearly in ruin. The other,
a similar building, stood near the old palace, and Mr.
Brown, a publican, is now the owner. They were
strong, two-storied, well-built houses, and were used as
inns in the old coaching days, when five or six coaches
daily passed through Tallaght. There is a tradition
which points out a place called " Talbot's Leap." It is
at the point where the little stream now crosses the road,
as you go up to the church. It is said that Talbot of
Belgard was away from home when the ubiquitous
Cromwell marched upon his castle. Having taken what
he pleased, Cromwell was retiring, when Talbot came
home. Being enraged with the sack, the latter pursued
Cromwell with what retainers he could collect. When

he overtook Cromwell's forces, he found that the Iron-sides were not to be easily overcome. He had to retreat with all speed, and, making for a drawbridge which was at this spot, he found it raised up. Impelled by fear, he jumped over the ditch, and thus saved his life.

The present glebe is about a quarter of a mile from the church. It comprises about twenty-four acres of good land. The house was built in 1825. The Rev. Mr. Lovett was the first occupant. He was succeeded in 1830 by the Rev. William Robinson.[1] The latter expended £250 in additions to the glebe-house, which remains a building charge on it. It is square, with a pointed roof, not unlike a tea-canister. The garden is celebrated for roses and apples.

---

[1] He was instituted on March 3rd, 1830, to the vicarage of Tallaght, curacy of Whitechurch, and rectory of Cruagh by Dr. Magee, then Archbishop of Dublin, and inducted four days later by the Rev. Robert Lovett. On the fiftieth anniversary of the commencement of his ministry at Tallaght—at Easter, 1880—the parishioners presented him with a silver tray and an address. In the latter, they placed on record the kindness and unwearying care, both spiritually and temporally, which they had experienced from him, who had been the guide of their youth, the participator of their joys, the sympathiser in their griefs, and the comforter of their old age. They acknowledged with thankfulness the purity of the doctrine taught by him, and the good effect of his consistent and blameless life. In August, 1887, Mr. Robinson was released from duty, and a few months later—on November 9th, 1887—he was called to his rest.

ANTIQUITIES.

THE Tallaght hills were formerly covered with the
rude burial-places of the prehistoric races of
Ireland. These were circles of stones, mounds, cairns,
kistvaens, pillar-stones, and suchlike, which are found
scattered all over Ireland, as well as over many other
parts of the world. The numbers found on the Tallaght
hills give colour to the tradition of its being the great
burial-place of the Parthalons, as before mentioned.
There is an ancient boreen, leading up from near Marlfield, at the back of Old Bawn paper-mills, to the top
of the hill. In winter it is the bed of a stream, in
summer a miserable stony path, with scarcely room in
some places for a cart. This appears to be the same
path as was trodden, perhaps a thousand years ago, by
the feet of those who bore the bodies of their relatives
to their last resting-place on these wild hills. Not far
from the head of this lane is a very regular circle of
rocks, on a mound; several stones appear through the
sod. I do not think it has ever been properly explored.
A little ridge runs for a few yards to the north
from it, and terminates in a round head, which is surrounded by a circle of very large stones. Two other
cairns, to the north of this, are very distinct, and are
composed of earth and stones. Cnoc an Terree is one
of the most perfect and handsome cairns possible.
Cnoc an Ralain was an immense cairn; but it has been

opened on the north-west side, for the purpose of getting gravel; and a great part of it has been carried away. A continued line of large stones appears round the sides. Another rath, near to this, has more the appearance of a sepulchral enclosure than a fortification. A little cairn near it is also quite perfect. The two cairns on Sliabh Foghail have been opened. One of them contained a grave, covered with a large flag, which was broken and carried away; but its supporters still remain, though not in their places. There were numbers of other stone circles everywhere over the hills. Several of the stones or rocks composing them have been quarried and carried away; and many of the ancient graves have been opened, and the cinerary urns which they generally contained have been carried away. These graves are seldom more than two feet square. Four large stones compose the sides, leaving a square aperture to contain the urn, and covered by a large, flat rock. Those which I have seen opened were about two feet beneath the surface, and were accidentally discovered by a farmer, when reclaiming a small patch of the heath. Each held an earthenware urn, with zigzag tracery, containing ashes, thus showing that incremation was fashionable in those days.[1] Numbers of similar urns are to be seen in the museum of the Royal Irish Academy.

There are, or were, several other moats or raths in the parish. One near Ballycullen was very perfect. It had a high, raised mound, which surrounded a circular spot inside, about fifty yards in diameter. A thick hedge grew round the top, and a deep ditch lay outside. This was levelled many years ago, by a farmer named Dunne,

[1] See Appendix D.

who, following the law of popular belief, of course, died within the year. The trace of this moat is still quite distinct. Another small rath, or burial-mound, is in a field on the right side of the road from Piperstown to Killsantan, or Glenasmole. There are some large stones appearing through the grass on the top. It does not appear to have ever been disturbed; and the superstition of the country people would prevent any attempt to do so.

At the edge of Featherbed Bog is another moat, called Cnocarmheibh, through which the county boundary-line runs. This moat was cut through to the depth of ten feet; but as the cutting did not pass through the centre, no grave was discovered. There are two or three other small raths up this valley. At the top of the Killinardan road there was another moat, which has now nearly disappeared; and over Killakee there was a small one on the side of the hill.

There is a large isolated hill at Knocklyon, or rather in Prospect Demesne. About half of it was removed many years ago for road-making. I do not think it was artificial. At Balrothery—a similar hill, about a quarter of a mile from this—about twenty-five years ago, there were found the remains of several skeletons about six feet below the surface, which was being removed as sand. On hearing of the discovery, my father and I went to see the bones. He popped surreptitiously one of the skulls into his hat, and brought it home. Soon after a deputation of the villagers came up to get back the skull to bury it. We had some difficulty in persuading them no harm should come to them from our possession of it. We afterwards gave the skull to the late Dr. Ball, the Curator of the College Museum. He said it was very peculiar, being small, very thick, and of the oldest type of the ancient Irish. The excavation for sand was stopped, and has never been renewed.[1]

This Balrothery Hill is the first of a range of similar sand or gravel hills that extends for many miles across the country in a northerly direction. The old road to Tymon Castle is made over the crest of this range, and follows the very winding line of the hills, probably to keep out of the marshes which once surrounded that castle, of which more hereafter.[2]

The nearest mountain to Tallaght is Seeghane, or the Seat. On the top of it is a large cairn of stones, about eighty feet in circumference. It does not appear to have been opened, and may contain a sepulchral chamber. About fourteen yards to the east of the cairn, is a grave, covered with a flag-stone eight or nine feet long and four broad. It has been moved from its place, and is broken. There is a similar grave about the same distance to the west of the cairn. The stone covering does not appear to have been removed. It is very large; and how it was carried to the top of this steep hill it is not easy to say. There are several other large flag-stones, nearly covered with turf, lying about on the top: they are probably also burial-places.

Following the crest of the hill for about a mile or so,

[1] A number of skeletons were found a few years ago in a sandpit lying to the west of Balrothery Hill. It is in a field called the Terrets, belonging to Mr. Stubbs of Newtown, on the banks of the Dodder. The skeletons were in separate graves facing east.

[2] Brewer, in his *Beauties of Ireland*, says that the village of Greenhills, between Tallaght and Dublin, claims notice for one of those circular mounds called raths. Here also, he mentions, there is a strong guard-house.

we arrive at See Finnan, a mountain considerably higher
than Seeghane, and quite covered with bog and heath.
There is a very large and perfect cairn on the top of it,
which, like that at Seeghane, does not appear to have
been opened. It may contain a chamber, like that on
Seefin,[1] which is about a mile further on, and is the
loftiest hill of the three. A great cairn crowns its
highest point, which is about 100 yards in circumference.
There was a deep fosse all round it; then a circle of
rocks placed edgeways, and inside smaller stones, piled
up about twenty feet in height. In the centre is an
opening, leading into a sepulchral chamber, about twelve
feet in length, and roofed with large flat stones, each
projecting further than the other. The rocks of which
the chamber is composed are of great size, and are
rudely fitted together. The roof of the chamber has
partly fallen in.

The use of these great constructions will ever remain
a mystery. The mountains must have been very
different when these cairns were made; now they are
all covered with deep turf and bog, and no stones or
rocks are to be seen anywhere. Formerly there was a
large cairn on the top of Mont Pelier; but a great
portion of it was utilized in building the house there.
The remains of the cairn are still to be seen. It much
resembles those already described, except that there was

---

[1] In the third century there was a military organization of the
Fians, or Fenians. Their leader was the renowned Finn mac-Cum-
hail (Finn mac Coole). Finn's seat or resting-place was thus named
from its being one of the hills on which this old hero is said to
have rested and feasted during the intervals of the chase, as his
principal amusement was hunting.—Joyce's *Irish Names of Places*,
p. 85.

no chamber under it. There was a pillar-stone not far from this; but it has disappeared.

At Mount Venus is a large cromlech, or Druidical altar. The covering stone is about twenty by ten feet across, and is four feet five inches thick. It is displaced, and one side rests on the ground, the supporting stones having fallen.[1] In a field close by there are numbers of granite boulders, some of them rudely carved. Another pillar-stone once stood on Tallaght Hill; but it has long since disappeared.[2]

[1] There is a coloured sketch of this cromlech in a collection of drawings by Gabriel Béranger preserved in the Royal Irish Academy. He thought the roof-stone was displaced by an earthquake in the seventeenth century, which was severely felt in Dublin. Borlase, in his great work on the *Dolmens of Ireland*, says that he came to the conclusion that the roof-rock had never been lifted completely on to the pillars.

[2] Mr. Dix, in *The Journal of the Society of Antiquaries* for June, 1898, describes a pillar-stone, or gallán, which stands opposite Mount Seskin in the loop formed by the new Tallaght road going round Tallaght Hill from Kiltalown to Brittas, and the old steep road between these places. It is a block of the clay slate of the district, and is seven feet high. There are five cup-shaped holes on the southern face.

E

HOLY WELLS.

ON Tallaght Hill[1] there is a well called "Tobar na Cluar," or the Ear Well; it was said to be good for the cure of ear-aches and headaches. Near Orlagh gate, about one hundred yards from the road, in a field on the west side of Mount Venus, is a well dedicated to St. Columkille. There are some very old thorn trees round it, formerly covered with rags, ribbons, and garlands, the votive offerings of those who came to drink of the water.[2] Beside the well is a large granite rock, in which is the deeply marked impression of the knee of the saint where he knelt to drink. It is said that the water of this well cannot be made to boil; but I never tried. Of late years, this and all the other holy wells in the country have been greatly neglected; their curative powers are not tried by the descendants of those who believed in them, and there are very few who would not prefer a pint of porter to a drink of the holiest well in the country. In the field, near the well, stands a large plain granite cross, erected about 1849,

---

[1] The proverb "Tallaght Hill Talk" appears to have arisen from the circumstance that brawlers and rioters, who had been confined by the Archbishop's court at St. Sepulchre's, used, when returning to their native mountains, to give vent to their feelings on Tallaght Hill, which was outside the jurisdiction of the Archbishop.—Wilde's *Memoirs of Gabriel Béranger*.

[2] See Wood-Martin's *Pagan Ireland*, p. 157.

with several others—some of granite, and others of
wood—to secure immunity from the cattle plague.

A spring, by the side of the road, near Tymon Castle,
is called the Fairy Well.   Close to it, is a small mound
called the Fairy Hill.

To the east of Balrothery Hill is a fine, strong spring,
formerly a blessed well, now called the Limekiln Well,
from a small hill near it, called the Limekiln Hill,
though no limekiln now exists near the stream.[1]   This
well is said to have supplied St. Patrick's Well, near the
Cathedral in Dublin.[2]   This might be so, for the

[1] This was possibly the spring to which Swift, accompanied by
Lord Orrery and Dr. Sheridan, made an expedition in 1733, and of
which the following extraordinary account appeared in many of
the Irish and English papers of the time. Sir Walter Scott says it
is difficult to know whether it is serious or ironical. " Dublin,
May 19th, last Saturday, the 12th of this instant, the Right
Honourable the Earl of Orrery, the Reverend Dr. Swift, Dean of
St. Patrick's, and the Reverend Dr. Sheridan, rode from Dublin to
Tallow Hill to take a prospect of the adjacent country. As they
were mounting a rock, they observed a stream running through the
middle of it, which fell into a natural basin, and was thence conveyed through some subterraneous cavities ; but they could not
anywhere discover by what secret passage it was conveyed out
again ; so that they concluded the waters were still in some
reservoir within the bounds of the hill, which must infallibly come
to burst forth in time, and fall directly upon the city. The Doctor
sent for a milking-pail to compute what quantity ran out, which
held two gallons, and it was filled in the space of a minute, so that
it runs in twenty-four hours 2,880 gallons. This multiplied by 365
produces 1,051,200, and shows the quantity that runs from the rock
in a year ; so that in three years, about the 15th of November, he
computed that it must burst the body of the mountain, and emit an
inundation which will run to all points of the Boyne, and greatly
endanger the city of Dublin."—Scott's *Works of Swift*, xviii, p. 130.

[2] Mr. John Martley in a letter to Mr. Handcock, says : " Your

stream from this well flows into the city water-course, which runs close to St. Patrick's Cathedral. A little to the west of this well there was formerly an oblong square, enclosed, containing nearly one acre, surrounded by a pretty deep fosse, the site of a village or castle, of which hardly a trace remains.

A fine spring, now covered over, in a field at the back of Fir House, is led through a drain into the Dodder, nearly opposite the third sluice on the city weir.

As has been before mentioned, there is a well at Tallaght Church, near the old stone font, which is now covered in.

There is a well near Killinardan, called St. Paul's Well, and another at Corballis.[1]

There was also a well on the high ground between Tallaght and Balrothery, now covered in, but an old thorn tree marks the spot. Many years ago a farmer named Ledwich owned the ground round this well.

---

statement as to the whereabouts of 'St. Patrick's Well' is at variance with my preconceived opinion. That opinion is partly founded on the fact that the old name of Nassau Street and the line of its consecutive was 'Patrick's Well Lane.' This I know from old title-deeds of premises thereabouts. I have also a recollection that Messrs. Cantrell & Cochrane laid claim to having this well on their premises, 2 to 4 Nassau Street."

[1] It was formerly known as Piper's Well. About 250 years ago Corballis was a flourishing town, and considered the first manor in the County Dublin. Part of the wall of the town is still to be seen, also the site of the jail and of the toll-house, where toll was paid on corn. Eugene O'Curry, in his *Ordnance Survey Letters* of 1837, mentions that there is near Corballis a field called the claish, the trench or furrow-pit, where a number of the inhabitants were buried during a great plague which raged there about 300 years ago.

He was annoyed by the people who frequented it, and broke down his fences; and he ordered his men to bring a load of manure, and to throw it into the well. None of his men would do this. He did it himself, and destroyed the well. As he was driving from the place, his horse ran away. He was thrown out of the cart, and broke his leg, which, according to the notions of the country people, was the punishment due to his crime.

———————————

PRINCIPAL PLACES IN THE PARISH.

BELGARD.

BELGARD, a hill close to Tallaght, was formerly the property of the Talbots, an ancient and noble family, whose members, for many centuries, have been distinguished in history. In former times, Belgard was one of the border fortresses of the Pale.[1] It was a strong, large castle, well fortified, surrounded by a deep fosse, very similar to Malahide Castle, which belonged to another branch of the Talbot family. Often did the lords of Belgard and the chieftains of Imaile contend in deadly combat. The details of these affrays would be most interesting if rescued from the obscurity of the dusty shelves and receptacles where so many unpublished records of Ireland moulder away.[2]

The Pale began at Dalkey, and, enclosing Kilternan and Kilgobbin, it crossed in a westerly direction to Tallaght. Thence it went on to Naas. See Ball and Hamilton's *Parish of Taney*, pp. 8, 237.

[2] In a poem entitled *Emmeline Talbot: a Ballad of the Pale*, Mr. Thomas Davis has given an account of the abduction of a daughter of the house of Belgard by a chief of the O'Byrnes. He relates how she was captured by the kerns on Glenasmole, and rescued from them by their chief Connor O'Byrne; how she and her lover were seized by her father's followers, and carried off to Belgard: and how, having released Connor from the dungeon in which he was confined, she accompanied him back to his tribe, and was married to him.—Davis's *National Ballads, Songs, and Poems*.

In 1637 John Talbot died at Belgard. He was a colonel in the army, and was buried at Tallaght. His son John Talbot fought in King James's army at the Battle of the Boyne, as the head of a regiment of cavalry, which he raised and equipped at his own expense. Having been included in the capitulation of Limerick, he effected the preservation of his estates, and passed the remainder of his life at Belgard Castle, which he much repaired and beautified. He had no male heir. His daughter, in 1696, married Thomas Dillon, of Brackloon, in the County Roscommon, grandson of Theobald Viscount Dillon, of Costello Gallen. Thomas Dillon died at Belgard, at an advanced age, and his son Henry inherited his estates. Henry's daughter Catherine married Dominick Trant, who, on the failure of male issue, became entitled to the estates, which thus came into the Trant family. Her son Dominick Trant married Margaret Bellew, niece of Lord Bellew of Duleek, and had issue, Henry Dillon Trant, who owned Belgard. He did not reside there, and leased it to a Mr. Cruise, who, being rather miserly, died very wealthy. Dr. E. Kennedy is the present proprietor.[1] The old castle of Belgard withstood the fury of the elements and the ravages of war for nearly 600 years. Towards the end of the last century it became ruinous, and partly fell down and was partly taken down. The moat was filled up, and the present mansion erected on its site.[2] The demesne is well

[1] Dr. Kennedy was succeeded by his grandson, the late Sir Henry Lawrence, Bart.; and his widow, Lady Lawrence, now (1899) occupies the place.

[2] Austin Cooper, who visited Belgard in 1782, says:—"At Belgard, near Clondalkin, is a small, high, square castle, with a house and other improvements."

planted, and is surrounded by a wall built by Mr. Cruise. It is badly supplied with water, being on a hill, and the limestone rock being only a few feet beneath the surface in most parts of the demesne. Newlands, formerly the residence of Lord Kilwarden, who was so barbarously murdered in Emmet's rebellion, adjoins Belgard on the Clondalkin side. This place was held for many years by a colony of White Quakers, who carried on their peculiar performances as long as their money lasted.[1]

[1] An underground passage is supposed to connect the Castle of Belgard with that of Ballymount. The latter is outside Tallaght parish. The ruins are very extensive, and the massive walls show it to have been a strongly fortified place. On a mound are the remains of a watch tower, with a spiral staircase, part of which was blown down in the storm of 1839. The castle was originally surrounded by a deep fosse. Béranger explored the underground passage for a considerable distance from the Ballymount end, and says it branched off in various directions. He found that it was well built, and thought it was originally an aqueduct for supplying the fortress with water.—See Wilde's *Memoir of Gabriel Béranger*. Mr. Dix, in *The Irish Builder* for January, 1898, describes the castle.

OLD BAWN.

OLD BAWN, about 100 years ago, was described as a large old house, with old-fashioned leaded windows. In the centre there was a small cupola, surmounted by a weathercock, which contained a clock out of repair. In each corner of the clock were the figures, 1, 7, 4, 7, with the words "Math Cr." The hands covered the remainder. Probably the figures signified that it was made in 1727, and repaired in 1741. Before the house there was an avenue of trees, together with several plantations, orchards, and gardens.

William Bulkeley, Archdeacon of Dublin,[1] as assignee of Sir James Craig, had a grant from Charles I, dated 5th March, 1627, of many towns and lands, amongst them those of Old Bawn, and lost, by buildings burned and destroyed there in 1641, £3,000.

By the marriage of Esther Bulkeley, heiress to the estate, on 15th April, 1702, to James Worth Tynte,[2]

---

[1] He was a son of Archbishop Bulkeley, and was a person of great virtue and piety. We are told he made it his diversion to improve and adorn his estate with plantations, and that from a rude, desolate, and wild land he brought it to a most delightful patrimony.—Blacker's *Sketches of Booterstown*, pp. 99, 159.

[2] The Tyntes of Old Bawn were descended from a Somersetshire family. The first to settle in Ireland was Robert Tynte, who came to this country about 1645. His son, Sir Henry Tynte, Knight, was returned as M.P. for the County Cork in April, 1661, and died a month later. James Worth Tynte represented Rathcormack, and subsequently Youghal, in Parliament, and was created a privy

this place became the property of that family, who are still the owners in fee ; and when the above description was written, in 1779, it was in possession of Lady Tynte. About the end of the last century a paper-mill was established here, which is still carried on, and is now one of the largest in Ireland. I visited this place in 1875, with Austin Cooper, grandson to the gentleman who wrote the foregoing description. We spent some hours in examining the locality. The dwelling-house has high pointed gables, and great chimneys, fluted at the sides in the Tudor style. The present house may have been built in Elizabeth's reign. The walls are nearly four feet thick ; the hall-door has a handsome porch, with pillars of round and square blocks of stone alternately. The greater part of the house is covered with ivy. The hall is a handsome, square apartment ; its ceiling is low, with large carved beams dividing it into squares. The walls are wainscoted, and there is a curious chimney-piece, with the Bulkeley arms over it. The dining-room has a similar ceiling, and is also wainscoted ; but the most remarkable piece of antiquity is the chimney-piece. This reaches to the ceiling, and represents in very bold relief the building of a great castle. Many workmen, beautifully modelled, from four

councillor. He died in 1758, and was buried at Donnybrook. His son, Robert, married a daughter of the 1st Earl of Aldborough, and died in 1760, being also buried at Donnybrook. He was suc-ceeded by his eldest son, James Stratford Tynte, who was created a baronet, and was General of the Volunteers. He died in 1785, and was buried at Donnybrook. As he had no son, the title became extinct.—See Blacker's *Sketches of Booterstown*, pp. 127, 281, 282, 286, 287, 306, and Burke's *Extinct and Dormant Baronetcies*, ed. 1844, p. 616.

to six inches in height, and in some places nearly projecting from the surface, are busily engaged with ladders,
spades, trowels, hods, and other implements of building.
Some carry stones, and one in the centre is working at
the great gate in the middle of the castle, on various
parts of which they are all employed. I remarked that
everyone held a sword, spear, or dagger in one hand,
while working with the other. Underneath is the date—
1635. It is a rare piece of work, and I think is intended
to represent the building of the walls of Jerusalem, as
related in the fourth chapter of Nehemiah. It may
have been erected by the aforesaid William Bulkeley,
son of Launcelot Bulkeley, Archbishop of Dublin from
1619 to 1650.

The dining-room is handsomely furnished with antique
furniture ; the staircase is well-proportioned, and the
balustrades are of carved oak. The house is a very interesting old structure,[1] and is at present owned by Mr.
Joseph M‘Donnell, whose family has for many years
carried on paper-making in the adjoining mill. The
mill is now the property of a company, of which Mr.

---

[1] Mr. W. P. Briley recently visited Old Bawn, and has kindly
furnished some additional information respecting it. He says there
is much carving on the beams of the ceiling of the hall, and that
over the fire-place there are two heads. The chimney-piece in the
dining-room is made of plaster. On each side of the design
mentioned by Mr. Handcock there are two heads emitting clouds
of smoke from their mouths. There is a winding stair-case leading
to two upper stories. On it there is a curious coloured window.
The banisters are ornamented with carved devices. In the room
over the hall there is a marble chimney-piece with pillars. The
furious driving of the phantom coach of Archbishop Bulkeley is a
well-known tradition in the neighbourhood of Tallaght, and the
coach is said to visit Old Bawn on the anniversary of his death.

M'Donnell is the manager. Several of the Dublin journals are supplied from it. The paper is principally made of Esparto grass and straw, with some admixture of rags. The Esparto grass and straw are first boiled for eight hours, at high pressure, by steam. The pulp is washed, bleached with chlorine, washed again, coloured with a mixture of red and blue, which result in a pure white. Then washed again, and brought into two great vats. Thence pumped into a distributor, from which it flows nearly as thin as oil on to an endless wire-webbing, the required breadth for the largest newspaper. This fine wire cloth, revolving on rollers, carries the pulp evenly onwards, drawing off the water as it goes. The pulp, growing drier, is passed over a vacuum chamber, in which, by the pressure of the air, it is so much consolidated, that it now leaves the wire-web in a soft sheet, like wet blotting-paper. It then passes over and under rollers, heated more and more until it is thoroughly dried and pressed, and is finally coiled on a roller at the end of the machine. Each roll contains as much as four miles—for papers worked by the Walter press. For others, a machine unwinds it from the roll, and cuts it into the proper size, at the rate of 200 per minute. The machinery is driven by a steam-engine of 200 horse power, and by several smaller ones, besides a large water-wheel, forty feet in diameter. There is also a gas apparatus, as the work is carried on night and day; very few hands being required.[1]

The plantations and orchards, which existed 100

---

[1] The mill has been closed since the above was written. The company were unable to compete with foreign manufacture. The place is now a desert.

years ago, have been nearly all cut down, only a few old trees remaining.[1] Near the house there was formerly an extensive deer-park. The walls which enclosed it in many places remain perfect. One of the former proprietors had a herd of reindeer, which he imported from Lapland ; but they soon died out, as the climate did not suit them.

A mill-stream taken off the Dodder at Kiltipper supplies the large pond near the house, and then is led along the crest of the hill, between Oldbawn and Tallaght, to the Haarlem mills, now belonging to the Messrs. Neill. When this mill-stream was first made is not known ; but it was probably early in the last century.[2]

---

[1] One of these, a large cypress, still flourishing, is called the "Informer's Tree," owing to the circumstance that a rebel, condemned to be hung on it, was pardoned for having given information. The stumps of three trees are still to be seen on which his companions were hung. These latter having withered, it is said on this account, were cut down.

[2] At the back of Old Bawn lies Ballymanagh. During the rebellion of 1798 it was occupied by some of the rebels. It was besieged by the soldiers, who killed one of the rebels and dislodged the remainder. They made off with the body of their companion, but left it in a field near Tymon Castle. There the soldiers, following in hot pursuit, found it, and, bringing it to the Castle, they hung it out of one of the windows, where it remained until it dropped asunder.

TYMON CASTLE.

O N the right-hand side of the old road from Balrothery to the Greenhills, about half-way between
the two villages, stands the old Castle of Tymon.
Built on an eminence rising from the plain, it forms a
conspicuous object for miles around. It is a small castle,
built in the same style as Cappoge, Cheeverstown, Mill-
town,[1] and many others, commonly supposed to have

been erected in the reign of King John. The lower
story is one entire room, arched over; the upper is

[1] See " Lesser Castles of the County Dublin," by Mr. E. R. M‘C.
Dix, in *The Irish Builder*, for 1897 and 1898.

similar ; the roof flat, with a winding-stairs in a projec-
tion, or tower, over the entrance. The doorway was a
small arched one, and the holes for two strong wooden
bars are still to be seen. At the top of the castle, over
the door, is a small machicolation, or place for pouring
melted lead or boiling water on the besiegers. The
lower part was inhabited by a poor family to the end of
the last century ; but the upper story was in a state of
dilapidation for at least two centuries earlier. An
Inquisition of 1547 states Tymon Castle to be then in a
ruinous condition ; probably the roof had fallen in, and
it was not worth while replacing it. King John granted
this lordship or manor to Archbishop de Loundres, in
recompense for losses to his See, and the expenses
which he had incurred in fortifying the Castle of
Dublin.

In 1247 it was constituted a prebend in St. Patrick's
Cathedral, which still exists, though divested of its
endowment. In 1306 it was valued at £10 yearly.

In 1552 a patent of Edward VI conveys the lands of
Tymothan, or Tymon, and all the tithes, in consideration
of the sum of £1,078 15s. 10d., to James Sedgrave,
with the town or village thereof, for 15s. 4d. quit-rent,
the contents being estimated at 230 acres. These, with
600 acres in demesne, he had power to create into
tenures, and to hold courts leet and baron. All were
subsequently included in the Manor of Rathfarnham.

James Sedgrave and his assigns held these lands until
they were purchased by Sir Charles Wilmot, who afterwards conveyed them to Sir Adam Loftus, to whom
several Church lands in Ireland were confirmed by a
patent, passed 20th March, 1619. In this were comprised, amongst others, the castle, town, and lands of

Rathfarnham, Old Court, Tymothan, and the plough-land of Knocklyn, in capite, by knight service, at 15s. 4d. quit-rent, for ever. William Conolly,[1] afterwards Speaker of the Irish House of Commons, purchased these lands, and they now form portion of the estate of his representatives.

In old times this castle was surrounded by marshes, which rendered it almost inaccessible. The stream, which forms part of the Poddle river, now winds in deeply cut drains, in a most devious course, through the fields round Tymon. It is easy to see that before the drainage was attended to, and these deep cuttings made, this stream must have flooded much of the surrounding country. The road to the castle is along the very top of the range of sand-hills before mentioned; and on one of them the castle is built. It is fast going to complete ruin. About half of it has been undermined, and has fallen, the stones being used for building purposes. Probably in a few years more it will all be level with the ground.

[1] See Appendix E.

KILNAMANAGH.

BOUT a mile to the west of Tymon lies Killyman, or Kilnamanagh, where were the ruins of an old monastery.[1] There were also remains of a church, and of a small square castle which stood at its western end. The castle was in good repair. A door leading from it into the church is now closed up, and the old oak door is in the kitchen of a house built against the castle. This door was studded with iron nails, with heads about three-quarters of an inch square. From an angle of the castle, a line of offices extends to the east. The back wall of these is built on the ruins of an old foundation, several parts of which may still be traced. It presents a very rude appearance. The stones are squared, and laid irregularly, without mortar. There are several pieces of porous grey stone scattered about the place, which the people called head-stones. There are many of these in an old burial-place close by, but which has not been used as such within the memory of man. A Mr. Farrell

---

[1] The Monastery of Kilnamanagh, or Acadh Finnech, as it was also called, was founded in the sixth century, probably by Patrician missionaries. The most remarkable ecclesiastic connected with it was Bishop Eoghan, or St. Eugene, a patron of the Diocese of Derry. He was a kinsman of St. Kevin ; and the latter, in his twelfth year, came to Kilnamanagh to study under him. Abbot Garbhan, the friend of St. Kevin, was of this monastery. It is often confounded with Kilnamanagh in Ossory.—See *Journal of the R. H. A. A. I. for* 1876, p. 89.

took the place in 1778, and at that time there were here
no marks of a burial-place.   When he was converting
this spot into a kitchen-garden, he found it so full of
human bones that he desisted from the attempt.   In
1830, when a son of Mr. Farrell lived here, one of
his workmen was digging a hole, and before he went
fourteen inches deep he came on a nearly perfect
skeleton, the bones of which were much decayed.

The site of another house may be traced in a southerly
direction from the castle.   The whole place was enclosed
by a wide and deep fosse, the greater part of which is
still open and full of water.   It must have been a small
fortified place formerly, when Belgard, Tallaght, and other
castles round Dublin had to hold their own against the
native Irish.   The road from Kilnamanagh appears to be
very ancient ; it winds along to Belgard, where it joins
that which leads from Tallaght to Clondalkin.   Proceeding
towards Tallaght along this road, we pass what formerly
were the Commons of Tallaght, enclosed in 1829.
Horse-races were frequently held on these grounds until
about twenty years ago.   I last attended them in 1859.
On that occasion the stand-house fell, and injured
numbers of people who were on it at the time.

The glebe-house of Tallaght was formerly reached
by an avenue from this road, near where it joins the
Tallaght road.   Near here a turnpike existed for many
years, but has long since disappeared.

Near Jobstown is Killinardan, where there were the remains of a small old church.   A little further up the road
is Kiltalown, the residence of the late J. Robinson, J.P.,
who built a handsome house here, in front of a very old
one formerly owned by a Mr. Carpenter.   The ruins of
another church remained on these lands, until demolished

in 1820 by Mr. Carpenter. He was a partner in the firm
of Bolton, Humphreys, & Co., of Dublin. Ben Bradley,
father of the redoubtable Tom Bradley, also lived in this
neighbourhood, at a place called Marlfield, near Kiltipper. He used to ride an old white horse, which was
as well known as himself. This horse had a habit of
coming to a dead stop when he chose, and no power
would make him move. It was said that Ben Bradley,
one night in a rage, shot this horse on the road, and
afterwards wanted to persuade people that he was fired
at, and that his horse was thus maliciously killed. He
tried to levy the amount off the county, but was not
successful. Another story is told of him that, getting
into some mess about money, he assigned his property
to his son Tom. He suffered a year's imprisonment,
and some not very flattering remarks were passed on his
conduct by Chief Justice Bushe. When he got out, he
asked Tom to return him his money, as he was now all
safe. "Oh, no," said Tom, "it is far better where it is."
Not a penny did the dutiful Tom restore to his parent.

Tom was as well known for many years in Dublin as
Nelson's Pillar. He dealt largely in money-lending and
bill-discounting. There was a certain balk, or log of
timber, which was always part of the value given by
Tom to evade the usury laws. If a gentleman wanted
£100, he would apply to Tom, who would cheerfully
advance £80 or £90, with the log, on the receiving of
an acceptance, well backed, for the £100. The log,
being of inconvenient bulk, was never handed over;
and "Tom Bradley's log" became a proverb. He
amassed a large fortune, and owned numbers of houses
in Dublin and Kingstown. His purple face was to
be seen at every race and place of amusement within

twenty miles of Dublin. In fact, he was everywhere, and always ready to do a little business. He was reputed a very good landlord, and fair in his dealings. Late in life he somehow got engaged to be married. Repenting ere long, he is reported to have offered the lady £1,000 to be off. She affectionately replied: "It is not the money I want, but the man." Poor Tom, accordingly, was married and done for. His residence was Ruby Hall, near Blackrock. Here he pined away, and died in a few years. He left an enormous fortune, designedly dying without a will. The lawyers had some nice pickings before his assets were distributed. His widow could have married again; but her grief for her dear departed brought on a habit of taking stimulants, which some way perverted her judgment. She could not make up her mind to accept her second suitor at the time he asked her; and her untimely death put an end to his wooing.

About half a mile further, on the left-hand side of the road to Blessington, is Johnville, formerly the residence of Mr. Roe, who made a very pretty garden, which sloped down the hill. There is a stream through it, which was led into ponds, waterfalls, and fountains. Its banks were planted with evergreens. Mr. Roe lived here for many years. After his death the place went greatly to ruin, and was for a long time untenanted. A Dr. Luther took it about 1854, and laid out a considerable sum in repairs, and in erecting Turkish baths. He expected that he would have been a rival to Dr. Barter, of Blarney. He had douche, sitz, vapour, and all other kinds of baths and contrivances for boiling out all diseases. Somehow the place did not take, though its beauty, the fine mountain air, and its contiguity to the metropolis were all in its favour. So it was given up in a few years, and it has been going to ruin ever since.

The old road to Blessington passed close to this house. Up the hillside the ascent was very steep. Many a poor horse suffered in consequence until the new road was made. This winds for some distance through a very picturesque glen, at a great height above the stream. It then crosses a lofty bridge, or rather viaduct.[1] The glen is well planted, and was formerly kept in nice order by its owner, Mr. Verschoyle. There were walks all through it, and a curious passage under the bridge, on planks fitted to iron supports, a few feet above the roaring torrent; while a waterfall occurred just below the bridge.

At Brittas, a little beyond this, are two large ponds, formed by damming up the stream, which ensure a regular supply of water to the Saggard paper-mills. These ponds are celebrated for the fine trout with which they are stocked. Mr. M'Donnell, who owned them, imported trout from the Westmeath lakes. These bred and multiplied, so that fish of three or four pounds were not unfrequently caught here. Great numbers of wild fowl frequent these ponds in winter. The stream which supplies them rises up on the Seeghane mountain, and is a branch of the Liffey. It flows through Ballina-scorney, by Pennybog, to Aughfarrel,[2] where, meeting a small stream from Butter Mountain, it forms the boundary between the counties of Dublin and Wicklow. It is here called the Brittas River. At Aughfarrel a weir or dam turns the greater part of this stream into an

[1] See Appendix F.

[2] Early in the century there were here remains of the castle mentioned in Lewis's *Topographical Dictionary*.

artificial cut, which leads it into the ponds ; afterwards it passes down the valley to the Saggard mills. It is then known as the Camack, or, in the old times, the Commock or Commogue River.[1] In Petty's map this stream was represented as equal in size to the Liffey, which it certainly never was. After passing Saggard, it runs through Corkagh, Baldonnell, Clondalkin, Drimnagh, and many other townlands, turning many a mill-wheel in its devious course until it at last reaches the Liffey at Kilmainham. The other portion, being the overflow at Aughfarrel, also makes its way into the Liffey at Bally-ward, the old residence of the Finnemore family. Here there is a heronry close to the house in some old ash trees. It is curious to see these usually timid and wary birds sitting quietly on their nests within a few perches of the hall-door, or attending to the wants of their long-legged brood, with the greatest unconcern as to human presence. Of course, they are carefully preserved from molestation.

Returning to the source of this stream, we come to Ballinascorney House, called formerly Dillon Lodge, as it was used as a hunting-lodge when the Dillons resided at Belgard. A large tract of the mountain here was also their property, and a walled-in deer-park, containing

[1] Eugene O'Curry, in his *Ordnance Survey Letters*, mentions that the name was unknown to the inhabitants until about 1835, when they saw it in law notices. The proceedings were instituted by the proprietors of the mills on the stream against Councillor Bennett, of Aughfarrel, who attempted to prevent the water coming out of his river into theirs unless he was paid for it. There is a tradition that the stream got its name from the fact that the men who cut the channel were paid in camacs, or halfpence ; but it is more likely that it is the diminutive *camog*, meaning " crooked," or " curved."— Joyce's *Irish Place Names*, p. 397.

about eighty acres, near the Gap of Ballinascorney, was, in their time, well stocked with deer, and was also a famous rabbit warren. This park still belongs to Belgard.

For many years Dillon Lodge was tenanted by the Bagenal family. Here Robert Emmet, on the breaking out of the unfortunate rebellion of 1803, came to induce the mountaineers to join his fortunes. Doyle, a labourer to Miss Rose Bagenal, then the occupier of Dillon Lodge, lived near here at Ballymece. On the trial of Emmet, Doyle stated that on the 20th July he had gone to bed rather the worse for liquor. On waking, he found two men in the bed with him. One of these was afterwards addressed as "general," and the other as "colonel," by a number of men, whom he found also in the house. The officers were both in green uniform, with yellow facings, and large cocked hats. The "general" was Robert Emmet, and the other a French officer. Doyle, being frightened, made off, and gave information to a Barony constable called Robinson, at Tallaght. Though Emmet was not taken on this occasion, Doyle was always called "the stag," or "informer," and his son is so named to this day.[1]

The day following, Emmet and his party took possession of Dillon Lodge. They greatly alarmed the Misses Bagenal, as Miss Rose Bagenal testified on her

[1] In a note left by Mr. Handcock, it is stated that it was Doyle who gave information to Major Sirr of Emmet's hiding-place at Harold's Cross. While selling eggs and butter there one day, he chanced to call at the house where Emmet was, and saw him cross the hall. Telling his son, Simon, by whom he was accompanied, to watch the house, he hurried in to the Castle, and brought Sirr out, who then captured Emmet. Doyle was given a pension of £40 a year.

examination. The greatest harm done was the consumption of all the edibles in the house. Emmet was subsequently arrested by Major Sirr near Harold's Cross.[1]

Gerald Tench lived at Dillon's Lodge part of each year for many years after his retirement, about the year 1852, from his office in the Four Courts. He had risen from a very humble post to a very lucrative one as Registrar on the Equity side of the Exchequer. He was paralysed, and drove everywhere in his carriage. In the house he had a wheel-chair, in which he rolled himself where he wished. Often when we were shooting over the Black Hill at the back of the house—which he took care should be well preserved, and which was a sure find for a few packs of grouse—old Tench had his carriage driven out over the heath to places where it was strange to see a four-wheeler. He watched the dogs setting and the shooting with the greatest delight. When we dined with him after the day's sport, he was wheeled in to the head of his table. He was a most strange-looking person, with a pallid face, marked features, and black skull-cap. He told many stories, and had the wine pushed round like the jolliest booncompanion. I never drank such Madeira or grand old port wine as he gave us.

After his death a steward of his, named Ward, lived in the Lodge until it was leased to the gallant Major Knox, proprietor of *The Irish Times*. Knox lived in great style here. Nearly every week in the season he drove his well-appointed four-horse drag, filled with ladies and

---

[1] In April, 1803, Robert Emmet occupied a house in Butterfield Lane, between Templeogue and Rathfarnham.

gentlemen, to his mountain home, and there entertained them right royally. He organized a band of twenty or thirty performers out of the printers' devils and the boys attached to the printing-office. He dressed these in uniform, and had a large omnibus, in which they were frequently driven up to the Lodge to play for the guests. The music could be heard for miles around, as they played their drums, trumpets, and fifes on the top of the 'bus, on their way up and down, creating great excitement among the natives, until the novelty wore off. Poor Major Knox overworked himself. He died too soon. Had he lived, he had a great career before him.

Captain W. Hackett recently purchased the Trant property here, and is now the owner in fee.

At the top of Ballinascorney Gap is a large plain granite cross, erected about forty years ago, but for what purpose I cannot find. The descent to the valley of the Dodder is very steep, and it is wonderful that no accident occurred in Major Knox's coaching days. The road crosses the Dodder by a fine bridge of one arch to Friarstown, formerly the residence of Ponsonby Shaw, brother of Sir Robert Shaw, of Bushy Park, Bart. He expended a large sum of money in improvements, in planting and in reclaiming the land. He ornamented the glen with winding walks, grottoes, and waterfalls. At the head of it he made an ornamental lake, of some acres in extent, by an artificial dam, about forty feet in height. Shortly after it was finished the dam burst, and swept away nearly all the walks and grottoes down the course of the stream. It was not repaired for many years, until a Captain Bayley took the place, and rebuilt it. A Scotchman named Watson succeeded him; but

he did not much care for ornamental work. The place
is now much neglected.

A little below Friarstown is Bohernabreena, where
there is a neat Roman Catholic chapel, built on the site
of an older one. Here a still older chapel existed long
ago. In front of the present chapel is placed a large
wooden crucifix.

Bohernabreena in old times was Bothar-na-Bruighne,
or " the road of the court," or "great mansion," one of
the five great palaces or breens, houses of universal
hospitality, for which Ireland was famed.

In A.M. 3970, in the time of King Conaire Mor, lived
the strong and brave chief, Da-Derga. The king was a
wise and vigorous prince, and established tranquillity
throughout the kingdom. Nevertheless, he had enemies.
His four foster-brothers were turbulent, lawless men.
He banished them from Ireland, and they took to piracy.
Some time after, having gathered a strong band of
robbers, they landed at Malahide. Thence they marched
on Tara of the Kings, pillaging and burning all before
them. Conaire, who was in Munster, opposed them ;
but finding the plains of Meath devastated, he turned
towards Dublin. Crossing the Liffey he made his way
to Bothar-na-Bruighne,[1] where Da-Derga welcomed him.
The pirates gave swift pursuit, stormed the king's refuge,
and slew him on the hearthstone of his host.[2]

So much for ancient history. In modern times a
strange scene took place near here. In the year 1816,
thousands of the country people were assembled on the
banks of the River Dodder, to witness an execution.

[1] Dr. Joyce thinks it must have been built in the Dodder, near
Bohernabreena Chapel.—*Letter to Mr. Handcock.*
[2] Tract by William Maunsell Hennessy—*Bruighean Da-Dergha.*

Three men, a father and two sons, Peter, Joe, and Billy
Kearney, were being executed for conspiracy to murder
John Kinlan, the steward of Mr. Ponsonby Shaw, of
Friarstown. The body of Kinlan was never found. It
was said at the time that it had been burned to ashes.
I have heard, however, that the country people knew
right well where it was buried. The evidence was purely
circumstantial. The Kearneys had been heard to say
that they would finish Kinlan whenever they got the
chance. There was a hatchet found with blood on it,
and hair that resembled Kinlan's. In those days, this
was sufficient to criminate the men. Lundy Foot, a
justice of the peace, then living at Orlagh or Footmount,
was active in securing their conviction. I believe they
were some of the first convicted under the then new
"Conspiracy to Murder Act." The three Kearneys
were brought from Kilmainham, surrounded by a troop
of dragoons, as appears from a sketch taken at the time
by an eye-witness. When the procession was passing
Bushy Park, the seat of Sir Robert Shaw, the felons
requested the carriage to be stopped. There they knelt
down in the vehicle, and solemnly cursed the Shaw
family through all their generations. Having thus re-
lieved their feelings, they went cheerfully on their way,
and arrived at a field on the side of the river, just above
a house then owned by Mr. Wildridge.[1] In this field
three gallows were erected. The dragoons were drawn
up all around, and in a brief space of time the wretched

---

[1] He built several of the houses in Harcourt Street. The walls
of these houses were so thin, that a story was told of a gentleman
sleeping in one of them who was wakened by hammering in the
next house. Presently the point of a twelvepenny nail was driven
into his head through the wall.

men were launched into eternity, amid the screams of the women, and the execrations of the men; for the lower classes were ill-affected towards the Government at the time. The rope for one of the young Kearneys, who was very tall, was too long. Galvin, who was the executioner, had to dig a hole under the wretched man's feet, which touched the ground until this was done. Old Kearney's wife was with difficulty restrained by the soldiers from attacking the hangman. Altogether, it was a dreadful scene. At last, when the men were dead, their bodies were cut down, thrown into a cart, covered with lime-sacks from a limekiln which stands close by, and brought back to Dublin, and buried within the gaol, to the horror of their relatives. Three skeletons were some time since exhumed at Kilmainham, which were said to be their remains, as the governor of the gaol lately told me. When the gallows were being removed, they nearly fell on Galvin the hangman, on which, notwithstanding the awful scene, the multitude set up a shout of laughter.

Above Friarstown is Piperstown, at present a straggling village; formerly it was more populous. The road from this to Castle Kelly is bounded on the left for some distance by the old deer-park wall, built 200 years ago by Speaker Conolly. A mile beyond Friarstown, we come to the well-known Monastery of St. Anne's. A few monks reside here, who hospitably entertain all who come, provided they bring their own provisions, or order them beforehand. Here, during the summer, and sometimes in the winter, a quoit club, so called, meets occasionally. Several of its members are more famous for their musical, facetious, or gastronomic, than for their athletic, achievements. The willing monks supply room,

fuel, and water, and many a pleasant evening is thus
spent in the pure air of the mountains.[1] A little further,
a winding path, sloping down towards the river, leads to
the Holy Well and ruined Church of Killsantan—that
is, the Church of Santan,[2] an Irish saint, or, according
to some, St. Anne. D'Alton says it was one of the
churches granted by Archbishop Comyn to the College
of St. Patrick, and confirmed thereto by a Bull of Pope
Celestine III, in 1191.

In 1216, Pope Innocent III confirmed it, with its
appurtenances, to the See of Dublin.

In 1231, Archbishop Luke granted this church and
Kilbride as an additional support for the Œconomy of
St. Patrick's Cathedral.

In 1306, this district was returned as "waste by war."

In 1513, the Prior of St. John's Without Newgate
demised to the Archbishop of Dublin thirty acres at
Killnasantan for fifty years.

An Inquisition of 1547 finds annexed to this church a
demesne of 100 acres. At this time Patrick Barnewell
had a lease for thirty-one years of a messuage and 100
acres of land, appertaining to the Rectory of Killnasantan,
together with the tithes of Templeogue, Knocklyn, Bally-
creughyn (now Ballycra), Glasnamucky, Old Court,
Tagony, Balmalyse, and the lands called Friarsland,
now Friarstown, at the rent of £4 13s. 4d. per annum,

---

[1] The monks have now left this place.

[2] In 952 *The Annals of the Four Masters* record the obit of
Caenchomraic, Abbot of Cill, rasping Sanctan. The church is
further identified in the *Repertorium Viride*, and was, no doubt,
founded by Bishop Sanctan "of good repute." A hymn by him is
preserved in the *Liber Hymnorum*, and printed in *The Irish
Ecclesiastical Record*, vol. iv, p. 322.

over and above the curate's stipend and repair of the
chancel. Soon afterwards, the situation of this church
being found inconvenient, a chapel was erected at
Templeogue, and this ceased to be a place of worship,
and soon went to ruin.

In 1755, Dr. Charles Cobbe, Archbishop of Dublin,
leased to his son, Thomas, the mountain, town, and
lands of Glasnamucky, Ballyslater, Killnasantan, and
Castlekelly. This estate is now in possession of Charles
Cobbe, Esq., D.L., J.P., of Newbridge House.

The ruins of the old church enclose eighteen paces in
length by five in width, and exhibit some architectural
skill. There are a great many gravestones in the churchyard, which is surrounded by a good stone wall, built by
Mr. Cobbe. The ground is considerably above the level
of the surrounding fields, caused either by the multitude
of burials, which for centuries have taken place here, or
by the church having been originally built on a raised
mound of artificial construction, dating from Druidical
times. We often find the old churches of Ireland built
on or close to Druidical remains, as if the sanctity of
the spot continued through all generations. Close to
the entrance lies an ancient font, of horse-shoe shape,
carved out of a granite boulder. It is about three feet
in breadth, by four feet in length, and ten inches deep.
Part of the back rim is broken. It is of very rude construction, and is somewhat like the old fonts at Tallaght
and Clondalkin. Many years ago, a gentleman residing
in the neighbourhood intended to remove this font to
his place, for a trough. Having with difficulty persuaded some of his men to undertake the work, they
put a chain round the font, and yoked two horses to it.
The chain first broke, next the swingbar, and finally one

of the horses fell and broke his leg, which put an end
to the project. The country people said that the ill-
luck was deserved, for this attempt at sacrilege, as they
considered it.

Further up the glen is Castle Kelly, a straggling
hamlet, which takes its name from a small, old castle
which formerly stood there, and a part of the foundation
is still to be seen under one of the houses. Eugene
O'Curry, who visited this place in 1837, relates that he
met an old man, eighty-four years of age, who remembered
the castle. He and his sister, Una, spoke Irish fluently.
Up to the beginning of the present century, very little
English was spoken in this sequestered glen, which,
until the last thirty or forty years, was inhabited by a
very primitive race, who had but little dealings with the
lowlanders. They preserved amongst them many of the
traditions of the once famous Glenasmole.

At the head of the glen is Heathfield Lodge, originally
built by George Grierson, King's Printer, grandson of
George Grierson, who, in 1709, had a printing-office in
Essex Street, at the sign of the Two Bibles. Among
his productions were the first edition published in Ireland, in 1724, of *Paradise Lost ;* Sir William Petty's Maps
of Ireland ; and other valuable works. His wife,
Constantia, was regarded as one of the most learned
scholars of her age. She was mistress of Hebrew,
Greek, Latin, French, and other languages ; was a good
mathematician, and wrote elegantly in verse and prose.
Her piety and domestic character were not inferior to
her learning. Her husband, through the influence of
Lord Carteret, then Viceroy, obtained, in 1727, a re-
version of the patent office of King's Printer in Ireland.
The life of his wife was included in the patent, in

recognition of her talents.   Mrs. Grierson edited several
classical works, which were greatly esteemed.   She died
in 1733 at the early age of twenty-seven.[1]

George Grierson, the owner of Heathfield Lodge
before the Union, is stated to have had an income of
about £20,000 a year.   During the shooting season he
entertained numbers of the nobility and gentry of the
country here.   It is said that he had six complete dinner
services, one for each day, and all were cleaned up on
Saturday, ready for the next week.   This George
Grierson was a very convivial old gentleman, sang a
good song, was very witty, and a first-rate host.   At
the time of the Union he received £13,000 compensation, all of which he expended.   He built Woodtown House at Mount Venus, where he had a wonderful
model farm.   He was very successful in gaining prizes
for his cattle and crops, but at an enormous cost.   He
had also a fine house at Rathfarnham, now the Loretto
Convent, and another house in Harcourt Street.   Notwithstanding all his wealth, he died several thousand
pounds in debt, which his sons John and George very
honourably paid off.   His three daughters, after his
death lived for many years at Heathfield Lodge, when
in this country.   They were great travellers, and visited
many parts of the world, at a time when it was not so
much the fashion for ladies to wander over the face of
the earth as at present.   They brought back numerous
curiosities to their beautiful mountain home, which
became quite a museum.   They altered the house into
a Swiss chalet, with a deep-thatched roof, and balcony

---

[1] See notice in *The Dictionary of National Biography*.   There is a
manuscript memoir of her in the possession of the Grierson family.

round it of carved woodwork. Inside the ceilings were
divided by beams; the polished floors were covered
with the skins of wild beasts, and antlers of every
kind hung round the walls. The tables were loaded
with curiosities. Outside the doors were mats made of
heather in blossom, renewed daily. The garden contained many rare plants, and magnificent rhododendrons.
The last still flourish, and are about the finest in the
county. The three ladies were respected and beloved
by all who knew them. The people of the Glen looked
up to them with the devotion of the old Irish to their
chiefs. In return they spent much of their time in
teaching and visiting among them, and helping forward
any of the young people who showed superior intellect.
They introduced wood-carving in the Swiss style; and I
have seen some beautiful specimens of the handiwork of
some of their *protégés*. Their brothers, George[1] and
John,[2] often visited them. I well remember the wonderful vehicle that John Grierson had built to order, for
going up and down the then dangerous road. It was
a sort of tax-cart, of great strength, with all manner of
boxes, nets, and other contrivances for stowing away
passengers and goods. There was a great lamp in front,
that lighted up the road for 100 yards in advance; so
that he could see in time whether it had been carried
away by a sudden flood, or whether a bridge had been

[1] He had six children. His eldest son was in the Bengal Civil
Service.
[2] He married a Miss Skene, a daughter of Sir Walter Scott's
friend, to whom one of the cantos of *Marmion* was dedicated.
His eldest son, George, was drowned while on a voyage to Natal.
He died himself in Syria.—*Letters from the Grierson family to Mr
Handcock.*

G

swept away since morning, as has sometimes happened.
He had an immense trumpet, which he sounded to clear
the way when he went up or came down at night.   He
and his brother George started *The Daily Express*.
They spent all their own, as well as their sisters', money
on the enterprise.   Failing just as it was established,
other people have benefited.   An accidental fire destroyed the beautiful cottage.   The ladies escaped to
a loft over a detached barn, whence they watched—
with what feelings may be imagined—the destruction of
all their treasures.   Mr. George Grierson rebuilt the
lodge on a plan drawn by himself.   His family is all
now dead—more is the pity, as is said.   Mr. Cobbe is
the present owner, and has the place in very good order.
He has built cottages for his tenantry all through the
valley, and they seem a comfortable class of people.

This valley of the Dodder is the once famous Glenasmole, or Gleann-na-smól, "the Valley of the Thrushes."
In *The Transactions of the Ossianic Society* many of the
old Irish poems relating to this glen are translated.
Several of these describe it as one of the hunting-
grounds of the great warrior and statesman, Finn mac
Coole.   Here, with his Finnian bodyguard, he chased
the enchanted doe, with his great hounds, Bran and
Sgeolan.   Here, as appears in the strange old Celtic
poem called *The Chase of Gleann an Smoil*, Finn met the
hideous wretch, who had crossed the seas from Greece.
She was the ugliest woman the world ever saw.   She
cast spells on Finn to compel him to marry her.   The
poem relates how she marched with an army of women
to Binn Edair (or Howth), and fought there with Blind
Goll the Mighty for three days, while fifty women-
soldiers watched the Finnians.   A love affair between

Diarmid of the Bright Teeth and one of the fair guards, with most stately, greenish, glancing eyes, led to the release of the Finnians from the magic spells. Conan the Bald cut off the head of the green-eyed girl for keeping them so long in pain. This done, the band rushed to the battle, where the ugliest woman was getting the better of Goll. In that fierce conflict they were cleaving each other to the bone. Most awful were the roars and bellowings that burst from the thunder-cloud of dust enveloping the desperate combatants. At length, Oscar the Noble makes a lion's bound, and drives his spear through the wretch's throat, and so ended her adventures. In another poem, *The Finnian Hunt of Sliabh Truim*, the manly, generous Finn slew the serpent of Loch Cartmor, the large serpent of Binn Edair, or Howth; the serpents of Loch Neagh, Loch Ree, of the refulgent Shannon, of Loch Carra, and of Loch Mask, the oppressive spectre of Loch Lurgan, and the Arroch, or indescribable monster of Glenasmole.

In the poem called *The Chase of Loch Lein*, the ancient name of Killarney, Oisin tells St. Patrick of all his men, and of their hounds. A great many verses are taken up in giving the names of the heroes and their hounds. He says : " I often slept abroad on the hills, under the grey dew, on the foliage of the trees, and I was not accustomed to a supperless bed while there was a stag on yonder hill. St. Patrick replies : " Thou hast not a bed without food, for thou gettest seven cakes of bread, a large roll of butter, and a quarter of beef every day." Oisin : " I saw a berry of the rowan tree larger twice than thy roll ; and I saw an ivy leaf larger and wider than thy cake of bread ; and I saw a quarter of a blackbird which was larger than thy quarter of beef. It

is this that fills my soul with sadness to be in thy house,
poor wretch." It is further related that Oisin, in proof
of what he said to St. Patrick, set out, attended by a
guide, as he was aged and blind. On arriving at Glenasmole, the guide called the attention of Oisin to a large
rowan tree, bearing fruit of an enormous size, of which
Oisin told him to pluck one and preserve it. Proceeding further, the guide's attention was attracted by the
immense ivy leaves overshadowing the valley; of these
Oisin also directed him to pluck one and preserve it.
They then proceeded to the Curragh of Kildare, where
Oisin sounded the Dard Fillain, which lay concealed
under a dallán, and a flock of blackbirds answered to
the call. Amongst these was one of immense size, at
which Oisin let loose a favourite hound, which, after a
fierce struggle, killed it. They cut off a leg, and brought
it, the rowan-berry, and the ivy-leaf, and laid them
before St. Patrick, to show that Oisin was right, and the
saint wrong, in his notions of the dietary of Oisin
while living amongst the Finnians. It is curious that
this tradition is still preserved among the inhabitants of
Glenasmole. I have heard the story related by two
men—one living near Ballinascorney, and the other at
the head of the Glen. The large ivy still grows on
St. Mary's Cliff, and Heathfield Lodge is covered with
it, some of the leaves being of great size.

Another poem, called *The Adventures of Amadan
Mor*, mentions the strong Dun or Fort of Glenasmole,
and that the Glen is full of witchcraft.

These curious old poems, translated by the Ossianic
Society, relate to events occurring in the very earliest
times, and, like all such legends, are partly fiction and
partly fact. The Glen must have been then a celebrated

spot. It was probably wooded up to the tops of the lofty hills which surround it, for many traces of trees remain in the bogs which now cover the sides of Kippure, Seefin, Carrigeen Rhua, and the other hills around.

In these wild woods the red deer, and perhaps the mighty Irish elk, found a secure retreat, until disturbed by the great deer-hounds of Finn, Oisin, and the other chieftains, whose deeds are related in these old poems. To commemorate the strength of the celebrated Finn, there is an inscription on a marble slab let into a granite boulder, lying at the end of the grounds of Heathfield Lodge, at the corner next the road. The inscription is as follows :

> " Finmakoom, one of the Irish
> Giants, carried this stone
> on his shoulder from the
> opposite mountain on April 1st,
> 1444—he was 9 feet 7 inches high,
> and weighed 44 stone."[1]

The inscription was placed here by the Griersons, but the stone, which weighs about a ton, was always known as Finn mac Coole's stone. Part of the tablet is broken, and only for the assistance of a man who knew the inscription by heart, I could not have completed it.[2]

[1] This stone has been thought to be the same as the one known as Finn mac Coole's finger-stone. The latter was so called from marks, which were said to have been left by the giant's fingers, when he threw it from the Hill of Allen to Tallaght.—See *Dublin Penny Journal*, 1833, p. 327. Dr. Joyce, however, is of opinion that the stone thus referred to was a different one from the one on which the inscription has been placed.—*Letter to Mr. Handcock of March 22nd*, 1880.

[2] The tablet has entirely disappeared since the above was written.

MONT PELIER.

LEAVING this ancient valley at Friarstown, and crossing over by Piperstown, we come to Mont Pelier, or Mount Pelia, as the country people call it. Mont Pelier was probably a fancy name given to this hill by Speaker Conolly when he got possession of it; but hitherto I have not been able to discover its Irish name. It is a prominent, rounded hill, 1,275 feet in height, and well known from the ruin on its summit, called by some "the Kennel," by others "the Haunted House," and by others "the Hell-fire Club-house."

This house, now ruined, was built by Speaker Conolly about the year 1725, shortly after he purchased all the estate of the Duke of Wharton, in this neighbourhood.[1] It was said that he built it as a point of view from Castletown, where his mansion was. When built, it could only be seen from thence when the sun shone on it, as the hills behind overshadowed it. It was then called "Conolly's Folly." Mr. Cooper, who visited it in 1779, says it was then out of repair.

Upon the top of Mont Pelier, from time immemorial, stood a large cairn, similar to those on Seefin and Seeghane Mountains. The limits were composed of great stones set edgeways, which made a sort of wall or boundary; within small stones were heaped up; and in

[1] It was previously reported that the Duke had sold it to Lord Chetwynd for £85,000. See *Letters to and from Bishop Nicolson*, vol. ii, p. 527.

the centre there was a large slab, nine feet long, six feet wide, and three feet thick, not raised upon others, but lying low, with the small stones cleared from around it. There were several other large stones; and about sixty yards south-west stood a pillar-stone about five feet out of the ground. These ancient remains have nearly disappeared. A great portion of the cairn was used in building the house.

I believe the house to have been built as a hunting-lodge. It stands nearly in the centre of an extensive walled-in deer-park. Many portions of the wall are still to be seen; it surrounded nearly the whole hill, and the park contained upwards of 1,000 acres.

The house consisted of two large rooms and a hall on an upper floor. These rooms are sixteen feet square, each of them lighted by two tall windows, almost eight feet by three feet six inches, commanding a most extensive and magnificent view. There are two arched niches at each side of the rooms, with large fireplaces. Over the parlour and hall there was a small loft, but none over the drawing-room. The hall-door was reached by a lofty flight of stone steps; these, with most of the other cut granite stones about the house, were taken away at the time of the building of Lord Ely's hunting-lodge, lower down the hill.

Underneath the drawing-room was the kitchen, where the jambs of the great fireplace, ten feet wide, are still to be seen. There was a servants' hall at the other side, and there were two rooms built out at each end of the house. There were also two small apartments in a return opposite the hall-door. The windows all face the north, for in the rear there are only a few narrow slits like embrasures. A semi-circular courtyard was in front with a gate in the centre. The walls are all very thick, built carelessly of rubble stone. The arched roof is of stone, as are the floors. It is said the roof was first slated, but the wind blew the slates off. The people said the devil would never let a roof remain on it, in consequence of the desecration of the cairn.

Squire Conolly would, however, not be conquered by devil or wind. He built an arched roof with large stones placed edgeways, and filled to a smooth surface with smaller stones and mortar. So well was this done, that much of it remains to the present, in spite of its exposed situation and of its never having been repaired. Indeed, on the contrary, every stone that could be taken was used in building walls and fences.

The roof was also much damaged in 1849, when the Queen was in Dublin; for a great number of tar-barrels were lighted on it, which made a grand bonfire, but split many of the stones.

When the old house was first finished, it must have been a substantial, comfortable-looking place. Now, alas! it is a mere ruin, each winter hastening its decay. It is only used as a shelter for cattle. The lower rooms are half filled with manure and rubbish. The stone staircase, that I remember inside, is all gone; and the cattle can no longer ascend to the drawing-rooms, as they used to do. The only way of getting to these rooms now is by climbing up the front wall to the hall-door; while the room in the return is almost inaccessible, except to an active climber.

The tradition that the Hell-fire Club held some of their meetings here may have been founded on fact. That mysterious and iniquitous assembly existed about the time this house was built; and a member of the Club then lived not far off.

Lower down the hill, about half a mile to the north-west, there are the extensive ruins of Mont Pelier House, formerly called Dolly Mount, once a grand hunting-lodge of Charles, Earl of Ely, who was advanced to the dignity of Marquis of Ely in 1800, in consideration of his vote and influence in passing the celebrated Union Bill. He received also £45,000 as compensation for the disfranchisement of his borough. This is, however, outside my story, which concerns Dolly Mount, or the "Long House," as it is generally now called. I consider the house was built by Henry, Earl of Ely. His first wife was Frances Monroe, probably sister of the celebrated Dolly Monroe, whose portrait, by Angelica Kauffman, once graced the walls of Rath-farnham Castle.[1] This lady, being the reigning beauty of Dublin, is said to have captivated the heart of Lord Townshend, the then Viceroy. A contemporary writer says : " Her stature was majestic, and her air and demeanour were nature itself. The peculiar splendour of her carriage was softened by the most affable conde-scension ; and as sensibility gave a lustre to her eye, so discretion gave security to her heart ; and while her charms inspired universal rapture, the authority of her innocence regulated and restrained. The softest roses that ever youth and modesty poured out on beauty glowed on the lips of Dorothea. Her cheeks wore the bloom of Hebe, and the purity of Diana was in her breast. Never did beauty appear so amiable a virtue, so adorned as in this incomparable virgin." After this paragon, this place was called Dolly Mount, which name it bore for many years. A man named Brady, whose

[1] This portrait is now in the National Gallery, to which it was presented in 1878 by John Henry, fourth Marquis of Ely.

father was alive when the house was building, told me
that the cut granite window-sills and door-steps were
removed here from the old building on the top of the
hill, and that all the men that could be collected round
the country were employed in the work. It would
appear from his statement that Charles, Earl, and afterwards Marquis, of Ely, completed the building; for
most of Brady's stories related to that nobleman. Lord
Ely employed three teams of bullocks in subsoiling, and
frequently rode up from his castle at Rathfarnham to
see how they were getting on. When the planting of
the timber was finished, he said to them, " If I live
until these trees are large enough to make a coffin for
me, I will make gentlemen of you all ; but I am going
to do an act that Ireland will ever rue." He alluded to
his signing the petition for the Union ; so this occurrence
must have been before 1800.

The house was two stories high in front, with bow-
windows on each side of the hall-door, over which were
the Ely arms, carved in stone. The rooms were lofty
and well-proportioned, with marble chimney-pieces and
beautifully stuccoed ceilings. The windows commanded
a lovely view of the County Dublin, with its countless
villas, and of the city overhung with a smoky cloud.
Beyond it gleamed the bright waters of Dublin Bay ;
and in the distance lay Howth, Ireland's Eye, Lambay,
and the coast-line—a glorious prospect on a fine clear
day. On each side of the house were large arched
gateways, surmounted by stone balls weighing about
five cwt.[1] On the sides of each of the gateways were

[1] In 1880, Mr. Handcock bought these balls from Mr. Carty,
and had them conveyed to Sally Park. One of them had lain for
some months in the stream below the " Long House," into which
it had been rolled by the boys of the neighbourhood.

long wings, formerly containing servants' apartments and stables. At each end stood a square three-story tower, with castellated walls and Gothic windows. The whole front was about 120 yards in length. Behind the house were extensive out-offices, kennels, barns, haggard, and all the requirements of a great hunting establishment. These were well walled in, and had a back entrance, from which a paved road went up the hill towards Piperstown. A grove of trees surrounded the house. On the slope of the hill, about 300 or 400 yards off, there was a wood, principally of Scotch firs and larch, which grew so close that daylight could scarcely penetrate. From its commanding situation and extent, it must have been one of the finest places in the county. Alas! how changed it is now. As the Ely family were absentees, this place and the old castle of Rathfarnham were greatly neglected. A tenant named Jack Kelly cut down all the trees, and sold them. The house with any care would have remained in good repair and quite habitable. The yearly tenant assisted the ravages of time to the best of his ability. He stripped the lead off the roof, and sold it. As the floors rotted with the damp, he used them and all the other wood-work in the house for firewood. He took the marble slabs of the chimney-pieces for thresholds and lintels for piggeries. In fact, he systematically destroyed the whole place, so that no one should ever live there again, and disturb his tenancy.

In 1780 the rental of this place and its farm was £570; now it is only £167. Its woods must have been a great improvement to the appearance of the hill. The only trees which now remain are at the eastern side, where the Killakee woods lie, and also lower down the nearly circular belt of planting which surrounds Orlagh.[1]

---

[1] On the 29th January, 1875, part of the manor, town, and lands of Rathfarnham, called Mont Pelier, and part of Woodtown and Killakee, portion of the estate of the Marquis of Ely, were sold in the Landed Estates Court to Mr. William Sealy for £2,750.

ORLAGH.

HIS house was built and the woods planted about 1790 by Lundy Foot. He was the eldest brother of Geoffrey Foot, then the head of the celebrated firm of Lundy Foot & Co., snuff merchants, of Westmoreland Street and Essex Street, in Dublin. Their snuff was used all over the kingdom, being as famous in its way as Guinness's porter is now. Lundy Foot had been called to the bar, but, being very wealthy, did not practise. He was an active, fearless magistrate, and was the means, as before mentioned, of bringing the Kearneys to justice. He lost his life in consequence. He was fired at subsequently in the County Kilkenny, and, though actually riddled by slugs, he recovered. Afterwards, on the 2nd of January, 1835, while superintending some planting at his place near Rosbercon, in Kilkenny, he was stoned, and almost hacked to pieces.[1] He was buried at Rower Church, at Kilkenny; but,

[1] Mr. John P. Prendergast, in a letter to Mr. Handcock, dated March 13th, 1880, says: " The first conviction I ever saw for murder was for that of old Mr. Foote, murdered at Rosbercon, a suburb of New Ross, Co. Wexford. The culprit was a strong young man of twenty-eight. He fully expected to escape; but a girl of twelve or thirteen was produced unexpectedly who had seen him running away from the scene, and convicted him. He was surprised—overpowered—and fell senseless in the dock. I remember there seeing Mr. Foote, Hon. Secretary of the Royal Dublin Society, prosecuting his father's murderer."

There is a picture of Mr. Foot's house in *The Dublin Penny Journal* for 1834-35, p. 381. Some particulars of the family will be found in Blacker's *Sketches of Booterstown*, pp. 73, 153, 355.

some two years after, his remains were removed to St. Matthew's Church, Irishtown, where a tombstone records these facts.

Mr. Lundy Foot, while living at Footmount, had the new road made from Ballycullen up to his gate. This is three times as wide as necessary, and runs parallel to, and about 300 yards distant from, the old road. He planted trees along this road and in other places; but he cut down these before leaving the place, not being granted a renewal of his lease at the former rent. At one time he sought to have this made the coach road to Wicklow; but, though direct, it was too hilly.

He got the beautiful bridge at Poulaphouca built where there was formerly only a dangerous ford. The name of this place was changed from Footmount to Orlagh in his time.

Carew O'Dwyer succeeded Mr. Foot as tenant of Orlagh. He held an office in the Four Courts, and was a great friend of Dan O'Connell. When his post was abolished, he was asked to state the average profits for the previous five years. He had sufficient interest to have this average spread over seven years. He thus included the time of the tithe war, when his income was a very large one. The last five were not worth more than £500 a year. He got thus a pension of £3,300, which he received until his death. He built the large banqueting-room at Orlagh, where on one occasion he sumptuously entertained Dan O'Connell and the Corporation of Dublin. Many Corporators slept in the ditches by the roadside that night, for the coachmen got drunk as well as their masters, and upset their carriages, making it a night to be remembered.

Mr. O'Dwyer has long resided in England, and Orlagh was leased for some time to wealthy Scotch people named

Brodie. Mr. Brodie died, and the place has come into the hands of a monastic order. Its members have added a story to the house, and have turned the banqueting-room into a chapel.

Opposite Orlagh is Mount Venus, a prettily wooded round hill. Here was a comfortable house, and large farming establishment, at one time owned by George Grierson, as before mentioned. It was called Woodtown, and is now in the occupation of Mr. Hayes.

At the entrance of the road up to Dolly Mount is the farm of Old Court. Its history I have not been able to trace further than that the name is mentioned in various patents and grants for the last 300 years. Here, in old times, were a village and chapel; hardly a trace of these now remains.

Mr. J. Magrane has an extensive and well-managed farm here, and a very comfortable house, with large offices. The adjoining farms are those of Ballycullen and Ballycra, formerly Ballycruagh, mentioned in Sir Adam Loftus's Patent of 1619. There is still a good house at Ballycullen, and on the grounds a Danish fort, already mentioned. Ballycra House is completely ruined, though it was formerly a good two-story dwelling. It once belonged to a certain Hal Smith, who served in the Yeomanry in 1798. He had a lease from the Conolly family of eighty acres of prime land here, at 8s. an acre. He was a dead shot, and rather a well-known man in his time. He lived to a great age.

The lands of Knocklyon, or Knocklyn, next adjoin. The castle of Knocklyon is probably about 300 years built. It is a small, square, three-storied edifice, with round towers at the two opposite corners. The towers are part of the house, which has been greatly modernized by new windows, doorway, and roof. Formerly there was an arched entrance, which led into the main room, at the end of which was an immense fireplace. The few sleeping-rooms were overhead. The name Knock-lyn, or the Hill of the Pool, is derived from the little isolated hill close to the castle on Mount Prospect, and the stream hereafter mentioned flows close to the front of the house. About 100 years ago it was owned by the Ledwiches; but for the past fifty years it has been held by the Magranes.[1]

Mount Prospect was originally a small farm-house on the side of the high road to New Bawn and Temple-ogue. About 1800, Mr. Hore and Mr. Birmingham, the proprietors of this place and of Delaford, then Springfield, made a new road dividing their lands, and shut up the old road. The house has been enlarged from time to time. Dr. M'Donnell, Provost of Trinity College, lived here for many years, and much improved the place, which is now very pretty, with plantations and ponds. It is held by the representatives of the late Captain Roberts, of the Ballast Office.

---

[1] In the charter granted by Earl Richard (Strongbow), Walter de Rideleford was the largest new grantee in this district. In this grant Clohlun is represented by Cnocklin and Cnockflyn, in later charters, and is apparently Knocklyon. Balmelise appears still on the Ordnance map as Ballymaice, north of Ballinascorney, which perhaps it originally included. Tachonicde and Chilmechetda form two of a group of lands associated with the still surviving Killininny and others adjoining frequently mentioned in connec-tion with Walter, and lying north of the Hill now called Mont Pelier, near Old Court. The names subsequently settled down into the forms Tagony and Kilmakethe. A much-injured inquisition seems to identify the latter with Killakee. Cruagh appears to have been given to Richard de St. Michael, about 1207.—*Journal R.S.A.I.*, 1894 p. 163.

SALLY PARK.

AT the opposite side of the road is Sally Park, purchased in 1796 by my grandfather. The house is very old. Apparently about half of it was first built and occupied, as the walls of this part are thicker and of a different style of building. The other half was subsequently added, thus making it square. It had belonged to the Earl of Clanwilliam before my grandfather took it. The earls of those days must have been content with smaller houses than at present. According to Archer's *Statistical Survey of Dublin*, my grandfather planted 7,000 trees of various kinds. The place is very well wooded, many of the trees being very large. There are trout-ponds, gardens, conservatories, and everything to make a place comfortable, many thousands of pounds having from time to time been laid out here.

The next place is Delaford, originally Clandarigg, a carman's inn on the roadside. The road then ran by the hall-door, out by the present avenue, and across the river to the paper-mills. Mr. Birmingham, who lived here about 1800, effected the change which has been mentioned. He built, also, two fine rooms and a hall in front of the inn. He made large fish-ponds, planted, and otherwise greatly improved the place, the name of which he altered to Springfield. He also procured the building of Templeogue Bridge. A tablet on the bridge once recorded this fact. The illiterate youths of the

H

village have so defaced this, that not a word can now be
deciphered.

In 1820, B. T. Ottley, then a Commissioner of Public
Works, took the place, and called it Delaford. He built
another addition at the rear of the old inn, which gives
the house rather a curious appearance. He lived there
several years, and his representatives have still an interest
in the place. Since then many tenants have had it, and
it is now much changed.

At the opposite side of the River Dodder, are the
paper-mills before referred to. These are very old.
In 1719, an Act of Parliament relating to the city
water-course mentions them as "Ashworth's New Paper
Mills;" so they were probably established early in the
last century.

In 1733, Thomas Slater presented a petition to the
Irish House of Commons, and received a grant of £500
for the purpose of paper-making here.

About 1840, Mr. M'Donnell owned these mills,
and expended a large sum in perfecting paper-making
machinery. He had a large steam-engine to supplement
the water-power; built an engine-house, and a lofty
chimney. The speculation did not pay, and the mills
have been gradually failing down to the present.[1]

Sir Charles Domvile, who is landlord of half the
country round, some years ago, at great expense, moved
a number of large evergreens from this place, and from
Templeogue, to Santry Court; but I believe most of
them died. He moved also a beautiful little temple
that stood on a high mound in the latter place. It is

---

[1] These mills have long ceased to work, and are rapidly becoming
ruinous.

circular, with cut-stone pillars all round, and a dome-shaped roof of granite. I believe it cost him nearly £300 to move and re-erect it. These and such-like amusements cleared out his noble fortune. In 1875 he became a bankrupt. At an auction, held at Santry Court, all the household goods, and the extraordinary collection of articles of virtu, engravings, and pictures—among which was a very curious one of the principal members of the Hell-fire Club—were sold, and scattered for ever. The picture referred to was bought, I believe, by Mr. Wardell, of Thomas Street.[1]

[1] This picture is now in the National Gallery of Ireland. The uniform of the Hell-fire Club was red, with white stockings.

FIR-HOUSE.

THE small, dirty village of Fir-House[1] is at the end of the cross-road from Balrothery Hill to the Bohernabreena Road. It is just outside the demesne wall of Sally Park, and is principally inhabited by stone-breakers. They earn good wages by breaking the whin-stone brought down from Mont Pelier for the roads. They get 1s. 6d. a ton, and can, if expert, break two tons or more in the day. Not many years ago, Saturday night and Sunday were spent in drinking and fighting. In my early days, no Sunday passed without one or more regular fights. The Fir-House boys, having drunk up to a proper pitch, were wont to issue from the public-house. Stripping off all their clothes except their trousers, they used to challenge the mountain boys, or anyone else. Many a hard fight have I seen from our shrubbery wall, which overlooks the village. On one occasion I was looking at a grand battle between a Fir-House boy and a Dublin pugilist. Many rounds had been fought, and the excitement of the crowd was at its height, when

[1] Mr. Handcock says that the house of this name was bought in 1800 by Mr. James Johnson. He sold it to Mr. Beresford Burston, who lived there about eight years, and was succeeded by his son-in-law, Mr. Smith. It was subsequently bought for a Carmelite Convent. The approach, which originally faced the back entrance to Sally Park, has been moved higher up the road, near to the chapel, which adjoins the dwelling-house. A wall has been built along the road.

word was brought that the priest was coming. Father Doolin, at that time priest at Fir-House, kept some kind of order in the village, and was the terror of evil-doers. At the sound of his name the crowd dispersed in a moment. The Fir-House pugilist crept up a sewer, and escaped. The Dublin man, who was told to run for his life, had just time to put on his coat over his naked back and do so. He crossed the wall of Delaford. Father Doolin spied him, and, bringing his horse alongside the wall, vaulted over after him. After a smart chase he collared him, and then and there gave him a fine horsewhipping, until he roared for mercy. "I'll teach you," said the priest, "not to come out here disturbing the peace of the town." This Father Doolin was a powerful man, fond of horses, and quite the old-fashioned style of priest, and was a great loss when moved from here.[1]

[1] The village is much improved since this account was written. The present inhabitants are orderly and hard-working, and wrestling matches and fights are traditions of times long gone by. Many of the cottages have been rebuilt, and the village no longer presents a dirty and neglected appearance.

SPAWELL.

BELOW the paper-mills is Spawell, an old-fashioned house of three stories, surrounded by a few trees, and close to the bank of the Dodder. The old road from Crumlin and Dublin bounded one side, and crossed the river by a ford at this place, before the building of Templeogue Bridge.

A little to the east of the house, in the centre of a semicircular hollow, was situated the once celebrated chalybeate spring, or Spa, which gave the name to the place. The slope of the bank behind was planted with large elms, all now removed. Near the well there was a great hawthorn, surrounded by a stone seat, the vestiges of which are still to be seen. The well is now covered over, and a sewer leads the water from it to the river, in which it may still be tasted. The entrance to the place was at the corner, where the road turns down to the river, and there was a plantation along the left side of the avenue, where the bed of the river is now. In 1846, the Government Drainage Commissioners straightened the course of the river, from the weir at Fir-House downwards. The river ran formerly under the old road, by Cherryfield, through ground long since reclaimed. A hundred years ago the rank, beauty, and fashion of Dublin assembled at this now neglected spot, for the purpose of drinking the waters, and the following particulars relating to it are interesting.

In *The Dublin Gazette* of 22nd April, 1732, appears this advertisement :—" Templeogue Spaw Well.--Patrick Daniel, at the Domvile Arms and Three Tons, at Templeogue, continues to hold the same, and hopes to give satisfaction to all persons who maketh use of the said water, there being a large room for the accommodation of gentlemen and ladies, as also good entertainment and attendance. A band of city music will give their attendance as many days in the week as the company and the Master of the Ceremonies shall direct, who are to be chosen by the majority of the gentlemen. The Well will be opened on Monday next, being the 24th of this inst., April, 1732, and to continue until the 1st day of September following if required. Those that have occasion for the said water are desired to send their names and places of abode the morning before, to Mr. John O'Neal, at the O'Neal's Arms, in New Street ; Mr. Michael Rainsford's, opposite the Horse Guards, in Dame Street ; and at Mr. Burnet's, saddler, in Christchurch Yard. N.B.—The waters may be had fresh every morning, at Mr. John Brown's, tobacconist, in Crane Lane." The Domvile Arms is now a farmer's house, the interior being altered to suit its changed circumstances.

There was a paper of eight pages published weekly about that time, called *The Templeogue Intelligencer*, which gave an account of the proceedings at the Spa. The paper is very scarce, and a complete set of it is not to be had. A few numbers are among *The Haliday Pamphlets*, now preserved in the Library of the Royal Irish Academy. The following is a copy of the first number :—

"THE TEMPLEOGUE INTELLIGENCER,
"No. I.

"'E cœlo descendit γνῶθι σεαυτόν.'—JUVENAL.

"Dublin, 1728—Printed by S. Powel, in Crane Lane, near Essex Street.

"I have been led into this way of thinking by a merry accident which happened yesterday at Templeogue. I had heard the world talk variously of the humours of that place—some commended the waters, and multitudes were living witnesses of their good effects; but many others as violently decried them, insinuating, at the same time, that those mixed companies were not altogether so good for young people. This contrariety of opinion led a mind, naturally so curious and inquisitive as mine, into an inquiry which party was in the right and which in the wrong. There is nothing, perhaps, in this life of greater importance to the well-being of a State or to the health and welfare of particulars, than the discovery of truth in matters thus controverted. I, therefore, set myself seriously about it in this case, believing that the prosperity or misfortune of our metropolis did, in a great measure, depend on the success of my inquiry. I went there early in the season, and offered myself as a subscriber. The stewards seemed to be surprised at a thing so new; but, in an agreeable manner disguising their uneasiness, they accepted of my subscription. Now, you must know, that I am a year and nine months past my grand climatrick, or in plain English, sixty-four years and nine months; my visage is long and swarthy, having a protuberance on the left side of my face, and a large wart on my nose, not unlike a wen; my left shoulder rises about four inches and a quarter higher than my right, which obliges me to carry my head, like the inhabitants of the flying island, on the other shoulder. As for my legs, they are not the straightest in the world, for the shin-bones rise out, and form each of them a kind of semicircle ; but in everything else they tell me I am as agreeable an old gentleman as you might see in a thousand. From my youth I have been an early riser, and found it highly contributing to my health ; so that the early hours of which others complain is no hardship to me ; and, what is pretty particular, I have not once in the whole season failed to be the first at the wells, and the last that left them, so that nothing could escape my observation. I always danced six country dances of a morning, and can without vanity tell you that the greatest belle has made the strongest interest to have me for a partner ; but I always took care that my moderation in exercise should be no injury to their health, and I was the only person in the house who could assign my partner to another, and demand her again without offence ; for there is an exact rule and order observed in everything, which no one but I can transgress without being excluded the society, and in danger of falling a sacrifice to the rage of our sanguine society, who pique themselves upon supporting an exact form and decorum in all things. I have been long considering what could be the meaning of these balls and this merriment, at a place which originally was designed as a resort for vale-tudinary and infirm people ; but I have at length learned from an ingenuous gentleman of my acquaintance, that it is the nature of all chalybeates to require a gay and sprightly humour, and a good deal of action, to give them a proper operation. I am very fond to believe that this very thing laid the foundation of the long-room, and established the weekly ball at Templeogue.   The waters of this place are specific in many disorders ; but they are more particularly adapted to the constitution of the fair and the young.   Many a lady, after spending a good part of her fortune on a vain pursuit after health in the apothecary's shop, has here at length, at a very trifling expense, found an agreeable vermilion for her lips, a snowy whiteness for her neck, and a rosy lustre for her cheeks, so that they are the most frequented of any within fifty miles of Dublin.   The hour of meeting is generally about eight o'clock in the morning ; but, the distance from town requiring an hour in the passage, the ladies must rise between six and seven to be there in time : and it is scarce to be imagined what good effect these early hours often have, not only on the health and con-stitution, but on the very life and conversation, of the fair sex.   I have heard an old aunt of mine say that before tea and coffee and late hours came into fashion, you might have lived a whole year in this very city with-out hearing an ill word of your neighbour behind his back ; there was little or no scandal, and the person who now and then attempted to spread a false report of his neighbour, was always accounted the most scandalous person himself.   There was no sitting down to dinner by candlelight, nor any sitting at cards till morning.   Every-thing was done in its own season, and the family was managed with an exact order and economy.   But if you examine these times, this lying-abed season, good lack ! how the world is altered from what it was.   The very rising betimes is, therefore, a most valuable thing.   The air and exercise in going to the waters, the innocent recreations of the place, and the returning again with a

good stomach, are better for the health, and more con-
ducive to long life, than all the learning of Galen or all
the aphorisms of Hippocrates. In short, from an exact
and careful consideration of the rules by which this little
society is scrupulously governed, I think fit to proceed
in my narration, to let the world know—such of them, I
mean, as, from too great nicety, have rashly condemned
the long-room—that it is impossible anything could be
more judiciously contrived, to prevent intrigues or
accidents of any sort in public assemblies, than the
little scheme of government already established there, to
which, for brevity, I refer. I have here met with many
occurrences, diverting enough, which, as opportunity
offers, shall be communicated to the public ; but, in the
meantime (begging pardon for this tedious digression,
to which my years have greatly subjected me), as I was
saying, I was thrown into this way of thinking by a
merry accident which happened yesterday at Templeogue.
You must know, sir, that amongst the celebrated dancers
of that place, there is one more remarkable than the
rest for a certain easy, natural, and unaffected manner of
performing a jig. She has a thousand other charms,
agreeable and taking ; but in this she excels. Jigs, you
know, have grown much into fashion of late, by the kind
reception with which such performances have met at
Court, and every good woman thinks her money thrown
away, unless her daughter can dance a jig.

"This has drawn a heavy complaint from all the
French dancing-masters in town, for Hydecar himself
has not taken a greater offence against the Beggars'
Opera, than this set of gentlemen have taken against jigs.
But there is no striving against a stream : the reigning
humour must be complied with, even at the expense of
many a fine French dance. Lucy, a young lady perfectly

well made, easy in her air, and genteel in all her carriage, would have made perhaps the finest dancer of the
age, had she not thought a jig her master-piece.   I have
often observed that when any person has arrived at a
remarkable degree of reputation either for singing or
dancing, or any other particular accomplishment, he has
never failed of making a hundred, nay, perhaps a thousand, bad performers in the same art.   We have all a
natural fondness for ourselves, a prejudice in our own
favour, that inclines us to think better of ourselves than
we really deserve ; and this often encourages to undertake things to which our strength and abilities are highly
unequal, and for which nature never designed us (as my
Lord Roscommon beautifully expresses it)—

> " ' Not remembering Milo's end,
>   Wedged in the timber which he strove to rend.'

"This was poor Lucy's case ; wherever she went she
heard of Sally's praise.   Sally danced herself into the
mouths, as well as into the hearts, of everybody, while
Lucy pined in secret, that she should all this while
remain uncelebrated for an accomplishment in which
she, in her own opinion, excelled all the world.   Urged
by her evil genius, away she hies to Templeogue, resolved
on victory or death, but so secure of conquest, that she
made no secret of her design, nor of the occasion of her
coming.

"There was a vast concourse of people.   Sally blushed
and trembled, and could scarce be persuaded to enter
the lists, till, wearied with importunity, she at last sub-
mitted to the entreaties of the whole house, and began
her own jig, which is properly so called, for none but
she could dance it.   The success of this bold challenge
put me in mind of an expression in Horace which I

thought so applicable on the occasion, that I gave it extempore in English to the company; and, as they seemed to like it, I will make bold to conclude this paper with it, in hopes that it may deter for the future all enterprising young ladies from entering into the lists with so dangerous a rival. 'Sudet multum frustraque, laboret ausus idem.'

> " 'In skilful jig, with painful art,
>   In vain poor Lucy plays her part ;
>   The power of mimic art whilst Lucy shows,
>   And all to art, and nought to nature owes ;
>   In vain she strives for glory in the plain,
>   Much may she *toil*, but she must *toil* in vain.' "

The few other numbers of this quaint production are much in the same style. For the information of those who wish to peruse them, I may mention that there are two numbers in vol. lxxxviii of *The Haliday Pamphlets*.[1] In vol. xcvi of that collection the following ballad also appears :—

THE TEMPLEOGUE BALLAD.

Printed at the Cherry-tree, Rathfarnham, 1730, and dedicated to the worthy Manager, Mr. Benson.

TO THE TUNE OF "TO YOU FAIR LADIES NOW AT LAND."

I.

> Ye Dublin ladies that attend
>   This place of mirth and fame,
> My song or praise or discommend,
>   As you approve my theme ;
> 'Tis you that make the poet sing,
> The subject 's but a trivial thing.
>   With a fal lal la, &c.

[1] The first, second, and third numbers were in the possession of Dr. Madden. See *History of Irish Periodical Literature*, vol. i, p. 303. The numbers in *The Haliday Pamphlets* are the fourth and sixth. There is also one number amongst a collection of Irish pamphlets in Trinity College Library.

II.

Those damsels that were used of late
   To rise when some had dined,
Now leave their toilet's pleasing seat
   For air that's unconfined,
On Mondays* rise by six, oh strange,
What stubborn hearts can't music change !
      With a fal lal la, &c.

III.

At breakfast, what a buzz is made,
   What scandal runs about,
What him, and her, and they have said,
   Or who's that that went out?
Such pratings round each table fly,
For one word truth, there's ten a lie.
      With a fal lal la, &c.

IV.

The cockscombs that officious wait
   With kettles in their hands,
And walk about from seat to seat
   To see who 'tis commands,
If smiles won't pay for all their pain,
Another time the rest they'll gain.
      With a fal lal la, &c.

V.

The fiddlers now, with sprightly grace,
   Invite them to the jig,
And pleasure sparkles in each face,
   With their own praise they're big.
A captive heart or two must fall
To Chloe's share, or none at all.
      With a fal lal la, &c.

* Monday, the day the company met at the Ball.

VI.

The rival queens,* with equal charms,
   Attract the standers' eyes,
And strike the soul with wild alarm
   Of love and deep surprise;
Yet raise, by their prevailing art,
The chastest wish in the foulest heart.
      With a fal lal la, &c.

VII.

How pleasant 'tis to view the fair,
   How sweetly we are caught,
With gentle smiles they spread their snare,
   We are theirs as soon as thought;
Who can withstand when Wemy's face
Brightens the lustre of this place?
      With a fal lal la, &c.

VIII.

The greatest crime 'twould be to miss
   A celebrated toast;
In future ages as in this
   She'll be Hibernia's boast;
Miss White for ever then must shine,
Whilst we revere all that's divine.
      With a fal lal la, &c.

IX.

Miss Sammy, whose exploits renowned
   Have run where fame can go,
With bays full oft she has been crowned,
   And praised from top to toe;
She loves a soldier's honest name,
By the major† she acquired fame.
      With a fal lal la, &c.

---

* Miss Pennefeather and Miss Vesey, two ladies equally amiable.
† The major was a celebrated country dance.

X.

Oh, could the muse her shape but span !
    And show her brilliant eyes,
But that no human creature can
    Behold them, but he dies ;
Blest as the immortal gods is he
The youth who fondly sits by thee.
        With a fal lal la, &c.

XI.

When all prepare their legs to prance,
    Each sex in rows apart,
They long to blend them in the dance,
    And show their hopping art.
A tune they want, and can't agree—
Moll bids them play " The Best in Three."*
        With a fal lal la, &c.

XII.

To shift the scene and paint the men,
    And eke the beaus also—
Oh, Muse, prepare thy flowing pen,
    With justice let it grow,
To lash at vice, but honour praise ;
Be that the subject of thy lays.
        With a fal lal la, &c.

XIII.

From foreign climes the worst of vice
    By Cunningham is brought,
To mention which infects advice,
    So artfully 'tis wrought.
His awkward grin and skull of lead
Shows Mother Dulness crowned his head.
        With a fal lal la, &c.

*Another country dance.

XIV.

Among the throng, where follies dwell,
　　Conspicuous Reilly glares ;
His silly tongue does sense expel,
　　His face his manner shares.
No more the vacuum shall confound—
Search but his head, no vacuum found,
　　　With a fal lal la, &c.

XV.

Fain would my song more courtly grow
　　When F—s—ter I name.
With wit like his to overflow
　　My lines, and raise my fame.
Words are too feeble to rehearse
Sufficient praise for him in verse.
　　　With a fal lal la, &c.

XVI.

The smoke of vice will soon infect
　　A youth, though well inclined.
Their glowing blood they should correct ;
　　Their intellectuals mind.
I speak to Boyle, and Hopson, too,
You should your parts with warmth pursue.
　　　With a fal lal la, &c.

XVII.

My brother Bard, whose honest heart
　　Still props our falling state,
And strives, with judgment and with art,
　　T' avert impending fate :
Who speaks so much, so little gains,
Just honour claims for all his pains.
　　　With a fal lal la, &c.

I

XVIII.

To him, O Templeogue, is due
  Thy praise and fame renowned,
Had he not been thy patron true,
  Thy well had ne'er been found:
Thy waters might have silent sprung,
Nor yet by him or me be sung.
        With a fal lal la, &c.

XIX.

His fluent speech runs smoothly out,
  Each word is fraught with sense;
The powdered fops are piqued, no doubt;
  With fops he must dispense.
Brown's an exception to old rules
That men of sense can't herd with fools.
        With a fal lal la, &c.

XX.

Ye Dublin Citts, whose thoughtless souls
  Incline ye to be blind,
Whose knowledge ends in brimming bowls,
  These, my last sayings, mind—
Where fops unnumbered pay their court,
Let not your pretty girls resort.
        With a fal lal la, &c.

Few people now-a-days are aware that Templeogue
was formerly a fashionable place. French, Swiss, and
German spas are now all the fashion. Lisdoonvarna,
where are springs of as evil-tasted water, and as potent
in its effects, as any foreign spa, is only poorly attended.
Lucan, once a celebrated spa, is now also forgotten. That
in the Phœnix Park, at the end of the Zoological
Gardens, had its day; and Grattan Spa, at Portobello,
after a recent slight effervescence, has again disappeared.

Templeogue Spa was frequented for several years.
Rutty, in his *History of the Mineral Waters of Ireland*
(Dublin, 1757), says: "Between 1749[1] and 1751 it
sank into entire neglect; and, indeed, this was not
owing to mere whim (as has been the case of many
others), but to a loss of its strength; for in the aforesaid
years, it had very little taste, and galls had scarce any
effect on it. It was limpid when fresh drawn, but grew
white on an hour's standing: it left something unctuous
on the sides of the glasses; it was but of a weak, ferruginous taste, of which it lost much on being exposed
three hours in an open glass; and tho' it was formerly
a custom to bring it for sale to Dublin, it could have
been of little value, except taken early in the morning
of the same day that it had been drawn; for I have
observed some of it which had been bottled and corked
in the morning, to have lost the ferruginous taste in the
afternoon."[2]

[1] In that year an advertisement appears in *The Dublin Journal*,
of April 25-29, announcing that the Spa will open on May 1st, and
that fresh water from it will be supplied to any part of Dublin at
twopence a bottle.

[2] Templeogue was resorted to for sport as well as for health. In
The Dublin Journal, of April 24-28, 1744, the following announce-
ment appears: "On Tuesday, the 1st day of May next, there is to
be fought, at Temple Oge, a cock-match, between the County and
City of Dublin, each side to shew thirty-one cocks; for two guineas
a battle, and forty guineas the odd battle. To be fought in three
days, wherein several gentlemen of the city and county are concerned. For the county, the immortal feeder, George Booth, of all
Ireland, is employed, who has beaten all English, Irish, and particularly French, feeders that he ever met with. For the city, Henry
Ellery is concerned, who was bred in London under the famous
and judicious Mr. Thomas Hackford, dancing-master as well as
cocker. Said Ellery's courage is much supported, upon a pre-

At the opposite side of the river from Spawell is
Cherryfield, formerly called Cherrytree, then a small
house beside the road that went along the bank of
the river to the ford at Templeogue, near where the
bridge is now. There were about eight acres of waste
land on the sides of the river here, all covered with furze
and gravel, with a rabbit warren. The river spread over
it when flooded. Since its bed was straightened and
deepened, this land has been reclaimed. Mr. Fowler
expended a considerable sum in building an addition to
the house, and in levelling and clearing this ground.
When Templeogue bridge was built, the road was
changed to run about a quarter of a mile to the south
of the house, instead of, as in the last century, running
on the north.

sumption for his education, that he can convey a manner of
hopping to his poultry, that said Booth had not an opportunity
of knowing. Each day's fighting begins at 11 o'clock in the
morning; and good eatables, wine, stables, &c., provided for
gentlemen that are pleased to dine at said place."

KILVARE.

THE next place to Spawell is Kilvare, now in possession of Mr. Roche. The demesne is surrounded on three sides by the river; the Tallaght road bounds the fourth. Mr. Geoffrey Foot, the brother of Lundy Foot, before mentioned, lived here in 1812. He built a cut-stone wall, at a cost of £1,000, along the river, to keep out the floods. This wall now looks very ridiculous, the river being many feet below its foundation, and never rising near it, owing to the carting away of shingle and stones.

In Mr. Geoffrey Foot's time, Captain Domvile, who then lived at Templeogue House, close by, built a wall about thirty feet high along the road opposite Kilvare, to prevent his place being overlooked. It is said that the Hell-fire Club often met in this house, for some of the Domviles were members of it. There was another house on the roadside at Kilvare, where once lived Archdeacon Magee, the celebrated parson of St. Thomas's Church, Dublin. His father, Archbishop Magee, resided in Kilvare about 1829, and some curious fittings were said to have been transferred here when the old palace (at Tallaght) was demolished.

John Sealy Townshend, Master in Chancery, lived here subsequently. He was rather an oddity: cranky, irascible, and penurious. An attorney met Townshend one day on Essex Bridge, enveloped in an old shawl, which he used to wear in his office, and had forgotten

to take off. The attorney, about to call his attention to
this fact, said, "I beg your pardon, Master, but "——

"Don't speak to me here, sir," said the Master ;
"whatever you have to say, attend at my Office at a
proper hour."

"I only want to show you this," said the attorney,
holding up one end of the old striped shawl. Master T.
was greatly confused, and was reported to have actually
growled some thanks.

He was of a saving disposition, and never spent more
than half his income. He sometimes gave dinner-
parties, and would pretend to fall asleep when he
thought the wine had sufficiently circulated. On one
such occasion B. T. Ottley, of Delaford, who was a
guest, and who was well aware of the Master's peculi-
arity, seeing the manœuvre, said, "Now, boys, as the
Master's asleep, I must take his place." He pushed
round the wine merrily, to the great amusement of the
rest of the party, and disgust of Master T., who soon
woke up. Ottley did not dine there again. When pre-
siding in his office, in addition to the old shawl in winter,
Townshend used to wear a parchment deed suspended
round his neck to keep his vest clean, with cuffs of the
same material, which had an odd effect. He died
worth over £100,000, but was knowing enough to dis-
pose of it previously. His representatives had therefore
no probate or legacy duty to pay.

Templeogue House originally belonged to the Talbots,
who, some three hundred years ago, seem to have
owned half the County of Dublin. In 1686, the lands
of Templeogue were mortgaged for £3,000, by the
then proprietor, Sir James Talbot, to Sir Compton
Domvile, together with several houses in Dublin. Talbot

espoused the cause of James II in the war of 1688, and, following the fortunes of his royal master, was accordingly attainted. Sir Compton Domvile thereupon got possession of Templeogue, the king being indebted to him for services performed in his offices as Clerk of the Crown and Hanaper. Having expended £3,600 in repairs, and in discharging incumbrances, he had a grant made to him of the forfeited equity of redemption. This grant was subsequently confirmed by an English Act of Parliament. There was a strong castle here in the Talbots' time. The lower parts of some of the towers still remain. The vaults under the house are of great antiquity, being wattled for the support of the arches—a proof of their having been built in early times. The two round towers at the back of the present house are of great thickness; they are built up inside, so that there is no access to them.[1]

On the site of the castle, a curious red-brick house was built, probably by Sir Compton Domvile; it had an immense window across the front, several gables, and other quaint specimens of Elizabethan architecture.

At the beginning of the present century the place was untenanted for a number of years, and became very dilapidated. At that time the demesne was densely wooded with fine old timber; there were several large ponds, and opposite the house there was a series of waterfalls, like steps, with statues on each step, all of which have long since disappeared. There was a waterfall near the gate, under a lofty Gothic arch. Its fall

---

[1] The house is said to have been a resort of the Knights Templars. It is also traditionally reported that James II slept there after his defeat at the Boyne.—Fitzpatrick's *Life of Lever*, vol. i, p. 323.

was about twenty feet. The water was supplied from
the city water-course, which runs along the highest part
of the grounds, and was diverted into these different
waterfalls and ponds. At a lower level it again joined
the course.[1]

The temple before referred to stood on a high mound
at the end of the largest pond, on each side of which
was a row of beautiful limes. It is said that an underground passage led from the house to the temple; but
I consider this to be a myth. There are several con-
duits and arches under the house and in other places,
for conveying the water from the ponds. This fact probably gave rise to a report, that the house was haunted.
This really prevented people living in it for a long time.
The old proprietors had the right, or perhaps took it,
of turning the city water-course through the channels
aforesaid.

When this water-course was made I cannot discover.
At one time it saved the life of a murderer. In the
year 1738, Lord Santry, being tried and convicted by
his peers for the murder of one of his servants, was
sentenced to death. His uncle, Sir Compton Domvile,
when all interest and intercession failed, declared that
he would cut off the water-supply to the city if the
sentence was carried out. The threat proved effective
and Lord Santry was reprieved.

This water-course, for many hundred years the principal supply of the city, could at any time have been

[1] O'Keeffe, the actor, mentions that in 1764 he went to see
"Temple Oge," the seat of Sir Compton Domvile. He says it
might well be called Oge, on account of its beauty. He describes
the gardens as delicious, and the cascades as being in the Marly
style.—*Recollections of the life of John O'Keeffe*, vol. i, p. 117.

wholly diverted at this place. It runs much above the level of the adjoining fields, being carried along between embankments, which it often overflows.

As I said before, the old place was neglected by its noble owners. It was taken by a Mr. Gogerty about 1820. He was permitted to cut down timber, in consideration of his repairing the house. This he did by demolishing it altogether. He was the builder of the present plain two-story house. It has since been occupied by several tenants.

Charles Lever, the celebrated novelist, had it for some years. He and five or six members of his family were often to be seen riding about the country.[1]

James Knighting—celebrated in another way, for having swindled the Great Southern and Western Railway Company out of thousands—lived here in great style on his ill-gotten gains. He was very charitable, and the poor about Templeogue blessed him.

Many others subsequently lived here. It is now owned by Mr. Murphy, but is not at all like what it was. Some of the finest elms in Ireland grew here— enormous trees. Most of these were blown down in 1839.[2]

Outside this place is a large flour-mill, now owned by Mr. J. C. Colvill, who has laid out a good deal in making it very perfect. Formerly Mr. Burke held the

---

[1] Lever resided in Templeogue House from 1842 to 1845. He was then editor of *The Dublin University Magazine,* and wrote for it (in 1844) one of his most characteristic novels, *Tom Burke of " Ours."* He also wrote in 1844, *Arthur O'Leary,* and, in 1845, *The O'Donoghue.*—See notice of Lever in *Dictionary of National Biography.*

[2] It is now the residence of W. Alexander, Esq.

mill. It was burnt down by an accident, and the present
fine building erected by the company with which it was
insured.

Close to the mill, and on the brink of the city water-
course, stands the old ruined church, and burial-ground
of Templeogue. The church measures about eighteen
yards by six. It is in complete ruin, and covered
with ivy. The churchyard, becoming overcrowded some
years ago, was surrounded by a high wall, and no
further interments permitted. Templeogue signifies
"the new church." About 1615, the ancient church of
Killsantan, near Castle Kelly, was found inconvenient.
This church was then erected. It could not have lasted
more than fifty or sixty years. I often wondered how a
graveyard was allowed here, for it drains right into the
city water-course, which runs through or rather bounds
it. In old times, however, people were not so particular,
and sanitary measures were not so much the fashion.

CYPRESS GROVE.

ADJOINING Templeogue Demesne is Cypress Grove, so called from some fine old cypress trees, which still flourish. About 1795, it belonged to the Jocelyn family. In that year the house was entered one night by robbers. The servants all hid themselves. Young Lieutenant Jocelyn, of the Royal Navy, who happened to be at home at the time, attacked the robbers with his sword. He put them to flight, wounding one of them, who had resisted, in the head and arm. Some months afterwards a man was taken into custody on suspicion of belonging to the party. Major Sirr brought Mr. Jocelyn to identify the prisoner. He could not do so, but said if he was the man whom he had wounded, he would have a sword-cut on his arm, and another on his head. His arm was bared, and there was a cut, which the man said he had got long before at sea, as he had been a sailor. He was then asked did he ever get a cut on his head, which was covered with a thick shock of hair. He declared he never did, whereupon Major Sirr ordered his head to be shaved, when there appeared a freshly closed cut. Major Sirr then told the man there was no doubt of his identity, and that his only chance to save his life was to confess his crime, and declare who were his accomplices. He did so, and some of them were taken and hanged. He also said that he had committed the great robbery at the

Castle of Dublin, on the 2nd of December, 1794. The office of my grandfather, Matthew Handcock, Deputy Muster Master-General, in the Lower Castle Yard, was then broken into. An iron safe that lay therein, locked and padlocked, was opened by means of skeleton keys. Debentures to the value of £1,750, and notes and cash amounting to that of £550, were then abstracted. A reward of £120 was offered, but in vain. This man said that he had bribed a sentry, who was on guard every fortnight. Admitted by him, he had taken impressions on wax, from which keys were made that did the work. He told where some of the debentures were to be found, but the cash was gone. My grandfather lost over £1,000 by the robbery.

After the Jocelyns, the Orr family lived in Cypress Grove for many years. They were very wealthy merchants, but subsequently failed.

The Duffys of Ball's Bridge were also tenants here ; and then the late Master Ellis. Charles King is now the owner. The gardens and conservatories are very extensive, and well stocked, as Mr. King is a great florist.

THE RIVER DODDER.

HE River Dodder has its sources in the chain of hills bounding the south of the County of Dublin. This chain separates it from Wicklow, and is known as the Dublin Mountains. Some of its waters, however, are drawn from lands lying near the summits of mountains in the County of Wicklow. The source of the Liffey is not more than four miles from that of the Dodder, so that they begin and end together, though widely separated in most places. Of the four principal streams which, uniting, form the Dodder, Dothair, or Dodere, as it was variously spelled, the first and largest is Mareen's Brook, rising at the back of Lough Bray on Kippure Mountain, 2,473 feet high. This runs down a steep valley, bounded on either side by lofty and precipitous hills, covered with boulders, diluvial gravel, and clay, nearly to their summits. It passes Heathfield Lodge, and flows on to Castle Kelly,[1] near where it is joined by the second stream, which rises on Kippure ridge, and, receiving another stream from Lugmore, shortly after is joined by the brook which descends from Seeghane Mountain, dividing it from Carrigeen Rhua.

Down the rugged course of this stream I had a toil-

[1] Ragstones, for putting an edge to iron tools; also clay, for making crocks and pantiles, abound on the shore of the Dodder from Old Bawn to Castle Kelly.—Rutty's *Natural History of the County Dublin*, 1772.

some walk one day, half carrying, half dragging a friend who, unused to walking on the hills, had become so faint as to be utterly helpless. Had it not been for two countrymen who were looking for stray sheep, I should never have got him home. As it was, we had to carry him, turn about, on our backs, for over two weary miles of as crooked ground as could be walked on. We reached at last the first cottage at the head of Glenasmole, where we left him to recover.

This stream is called the Cataract of the Rowan Tree. It flows in a narrow and tortuous course, through rocks and boulders, forming many a picturesque cascade and pool. Leaving the foot of St. Mary's Cliff, where grows the giant ivy, celebrated in the Ossianic Poems before mentioned, it flows under many a small rowan tree, no doubt lineal descendants of that which, in Oisin's time, bore berries larger than St. Patrick's loaves. Lower down the Glenasmole Valley, the Dodder receives little streamlets from Glassmullaun, and one from the Holy Well of Killsantan, another at Ballymore Finn, and another at Allagour. Passing through the village of Glassamucky, it reaches the end of the valley at Friars-town, or Bohernabreena. The river falls about 350 feet in the first two miles, the banks being mostly formed of gravel and boulders, and the detritus of granite, calca-reous, schistose, and trap rocks, embedded in granite sand and argillaceous clay. In one or two spots the banks are cemented with a hard conglomerate, by the infiltration of water charged with the carbonate of lime, which has formed aragonite in the interstices of the gravel. Some enormous blocks of this conglomerate lie at the foot of the cliff, from which they have fallen. Here it was proposed, about thirty years ago, to make some large reservoirs, by which the flood waters would be retained, and not only a regular supply sent to the mills below, but about 110 acres of good land, liable to erosion and flooding, would be made available, and about seventy acres of barren shingle rendered productive of valuable crops, instead of stones and sand, useful only for road-making. These plans were, unfortunately, not carried out.[1] This spot was also spoken of at the time the Vartry scheme was carried out for supplying water to the city at high pressure. It would have answered quite as well as the Vartry; but there were no engineering difficulties to be overcome, and it would not have cost a tithe of the Vartry works. The project was shelved, and not quite a million expended on the Vartry, which has been, I must say, a successful plan for so far. Anyone looking at the valley above Bohernabreena Bridge, would say that a finer reservoir could not be found. The river flows through a narrow cut in a natural embankment, extending across the end of the valley, which could have easily been stopped up.[2]

The total catchment basin of the Dodder is about fifty-five square miles, of which about twenty-two and a quarter are mountain, and thirty-two and a quarter plain, or of moderate inclination. The rapid floods, caused by the steepness of the sides of the catchment basin, carry

[1] See Robert Malet's report on the subject, printed in 1844.

[2] In 1877 it was decided to make use of the waters of the Dodder for the supply of the populous township of Rathmines and Rathgar. The works have been carried out with the greatest success, and a supply of 3,000,000 gallons daily has been obtained for the use of the township. See Description of the "Rathmines and Rathgar Township Waterworks," by A. W. N. Tyrrell, M. INST. C.E.

down great quantities of mud and shingle. The latter is now mostly deposited above the city weir at Fir-House, forming an inexhaustible supply of rather bad road material. Probably not less than 4,000 tons are, and have been for many years, annually removed. The consequence is, that the bed of the river from below Kiltipper has been lowered several feet, the river now running in a deep channel, in some places reaching to the rock, but principally cut in the blue clay. I have seen the roots and part of the stems of trees, apparently *in situ*, in a place where the channel is pretty deeply cut, on a turfy soil, bared by the floods. It is hard to understand how this happened, except that there was a deeper channel, of which there is no present trace, in which the river formerly ran.

Many have been the attempts, and large the sums of money spent by various riparian proprietors in striving to reclaim portions of the extensive strands between Kiltipper and Fir-House. Costly walls have been built, and as often undermined and levelled by this turbulent river; bridges have been swept away, and new tracts of ground devastated. Of late years, owing to the channel having become so deep, the river has become more tractable, and has not done so much damage.

To return to Friarstown; the river here receives the stream from Piperstown, and another from Ballinascorney. Here was at one time a small corn-mill, worked, I should say, by the Piperstown stream. It has long since gone to decay.

Below this, is Bohernabreena Bridge, built about forty years ago, across a very narrow part of the river, where formerly there was a plank thrown over it as a foot-bridge, at a spot called the Sheep-hole, which is a deep eddy under a steep rock. It is much used for washing sheep, and abounds with fine trout, which are fished for most assiduously all the season by Dubliners. The trout are so experienced, that they know every fly or artificial bait in Martin Kelly's, and are not to be taken by fair means. Sometimes the natives put in quick-lime when the river is low, and thus kill numbers. It is soon refilled, for the upper waters above Castle Kelly are preserved, and abound with small trout. The other kinds of fish in this river are eels, sticklebacks, locheen or gudgeon, and minnows. The last were not known in the river until about twenty years ago, when we brought a number from Lough Dan to our ponds, from whence they spread into the river, and are now to be found in myriads.

A little below Friarstown is a weir, formerly made of loose stones and sods, requiring renewal after every flood. This diverts most of the river into a mill-race, which for some distance follows its course under the left bank. Here are the remains of what was called the parchment-mill. Hardly a trace of it exists. The water which supplied it must have been taken from the Ballinascorney stream. This stands high above the mill-race, which is carried along in a very rude channel, full of leaks and overflows, staunched, as occasion requires, with sods and boards. When a flood came down, the weir was swept away, and all the mills below to Fir-House left idle, until it was repaired

Below Kiltipper, or Diana, as this spot is sometimes called, the race is led across the fields into Old Bawn, where it works the paper-mills. The main course of the river below this weir spreads as the valley widens. On the steep right bank under Friarstown, there is a remark-

K

able bed of tufa close to what was once a picturesque
cottage called Ferndale, now in ruin. A spring, having
a quantity of carbonate of lime in solution, trickles
through the moss and grass, and, encrusting the delicate
stems and leaves in a short space of time, turns the
whole into a beautiful petrifaction, the upper portion
being living moss, while underneath it is hard stone.
Some of the specimens which I have taken from it rival
the finest coral. Every leaf and fibre of the delicate
moss is transformed to durable stone. After thirty years'
exposure to the weather, these are as perfect as when
removed. Some of the blocks weighed several hundredweights, and are unrivalled for rockery work. I do not
think such specimens are now to be had.

A little below this, the river passes an old house on
the left bank, formerly belonging to Mr. Wildridge.
Near this is the spot where the Kearneys were hanged.
This house is now in possession of the representatives of
Billy O'Neill, some time since a noted Dublin under-
taker. The bed of the river here is now very deep.
The floods have cut down to the blue clay, where, about
thirty years ago, there were a road and ford across it,
now impassable.

A quarter of a mile below here is Old Bawn Bridge,
a fine arch of one span, built about 1840. There was a
bridge of three arches on the same spot before ; but it
only stood about forty years, when, becoming undermined, it had to be taken down. The present one is
not likely to last as long. Its foundations are already
exposed. Unless some care is taken, down it must
come. Below this the bed of the river becomes very
wide, and there are acres of shingle and waste land
extending to the City Weir at Fir-House.

Half a mile below Old Bawn Bridge, the mill-race before mentioned joins the course of the main river, after turning the wheels of Messrs. Neill's Mills, at Haarlem. The race does not flow into the river, but runs parallel under the bank for some distance, until it takes a turn to the left under what appears to have once been the bank of the river, but it is now a long way from it. The race is used in working the Boldbrook Cardboard and Packing Paper Mills, belonging to the Messrs. Boardman. Here it is joined by the Tallaght Brook, and soon after it flows into the main stream under Mr. Stubbs's farm.

On the opposite bank of the river is Killininy, an old house once owned by a Mr. Johnstone. Next to it is Sporting Hall, formerly called the Moorhouse, once a good residence, but now nearly a ruin. The village of Upper Fir-House divides these lands from the convent, between which and Balrothery Hill, on the opposite side, the river here reaches the City Weir.

The several Acts of Parliament relating to the city water-course all say it existed from time immemorial. In 1308, John Le Decer, then Mayor of Dublin, cleared the city water-course, and embanked it with stone; but whether the weir was then, or previously built, is uncertain.[1] The whole river is here turned

---

[1] In Mr. H. F. Berry's exhaustive paper on "The Water Supply of Ancient Dublin" (*Journal of the Royal Society of Antiquaries of Ireland*, for 1891, p. 557), he says the citizens of Dublin became indebted to this source for their supply as far back as 1244, and on it they continued to depend until 1775. In the map of Tallaght Parish in the Down Survey made in 1656, the "water that supplieth Dublin" is described at one place as "the tongue." In 1456 John Pylle, of Templeogue, was sworn to keep the

into the city water-course, except in floods, when the overflow runs down the main channel in a narrow, deep, and
nearly straight course to Kilvare. Thirty years ago it
was easy to drive across below the weir : in fact, it was
the main road to Tallaght and the Greenhills. Now
there is a precipitous bank of twenty feet deep on each
side, and it is impassable. For many years the only
way of crossing from Fir-House during a flood was by
the dangerous one of wading along the top of the
weir. The water rushes with great force, although of
little depth ; and if the foot slipped, the consequences
might be fatal.

Long ago there was a wooden foot-bridge put up below
the weir by subscription ; but this was soon swept away
in a flood, and the planks floated down to Ringsend.
About fifteen years ago, a neat iron lattice-bridge was
put up for foot-passengers, which is still in good order.
It is twenty feet above the bed of the river, and about
the level of the old road. Below the weir, the river
receives two small streams from Mont Pelier ; and
passing in front of the paper-mills, where there was
another ford, it spread over a wide bed of shingle
opposite Spawell. This was reclaimed by Mr. Fowler,
of Cherryfield, and the river runs in a straight, deep
course to Kilvare.

Kilvare is here surrounded on three sides by the river.
It receives a stream at a spot called Pussy's Leap,
and soon after passes Templeogue Bridge, built, as

water, and bring it as far as the cistern of the city. In 1491,
one Walsh was to have conduct of the water from " the head " at
the Dodder to the " tongue and harbour." From the " tongue to
the cistern " the water was " to be kept as of old time."

before noticed, by Mr. Bermingham. This means he
was the overseer, and got the credit of it, like "the noble
lord who, of his great bounty, built a bridge at the
expense of the county." Templeogue Bridge some years
ago was nearly undermined; but there is now a substantial weir or dam built below it. This, as long as
it lasts, will keep it safe.[1]

The river now runs between very steep clay banks,
twenty or thirty feet high, in a very winding course to
Bushy Park, the late Sir Robert Shaw's demesne. Sir
Robert, taking advantage of a shelf of slaty clay that
crossed the river, made a small weir, to turn some of
the water into ponds in his pleasure-grounds. This weir
is now demolished, and in floods a tremendous current
runs through a narrow cleft in its ruins. It leaves many
testimonies of its prowess by tearing down walls and
buttresses of enormous strength, reaching Rathfarnham.
Here we must leave it, and return to Kiltipper and
follow the mill-race. This, having assisted in the
making of newspapers at Old Bawn Mills, is brought
along the crest of a rising ground to the Haarlem Mills,

[1] A house called Riversdale stands at the corner, where Butterfield
Lane joins the road from Fir-House to Templeogue Bridge. It
was built about 1840 by Mr. Hughes. It was occupied subsequently by Mr. W. Pigeon, J.P., and afterwards by Dr. Noble
Seward, for many years the dispensary officer of Tallaght district.
He was a great ventriloquist. By the exercise of his power, on one
occasion, he induced some people in Dublin to tear up the pavement, under the belief that there was a man, who had escaped
from prison, in the sewer underneath. The scene is graphically
described by Lever in *Charles O'Malley*. Dr. Seward, shortly
before his death, in 1877, told his friends that Lever's account was
founded on fact, and that the occurrence had really happened. See
Fitzpatrick's *Life of Lever*, vol. i, p. 124.

where formerly there was the most celebrated bleach
green in Ireland.

In 1776, the mills were worked by Haarlem & Company, from whence the present name. They were calico
printers. In 1813 Mr. Bewley was one of the prin-
cipals. He was uncle to the late Samuel Bewley, so
well known for his extensive benevolence. In 1812,
Mrs. Elizabeth Dawson left by her will an annuity of £6
per annum to Anne Bewley in trust, while she should
reside here, for the poor of Haarlem. I wonder what
has become of it? Here are now four mills, owned by
Messrs. Neill—one of them being woollen and the others
flour mills. The next mill is that at Boldbrook, owned
by Messrs. Boardman, and the next the old paper-mills
at Fir-House, before mentioned. The river here joins
the city water-course. The citizens are fortunate that
they are not now dependent on it, for it is so polluted
by the paper-making that it has become poisonous, and
cattle and horses have died from drinking it. Sometimes it is the same colour as porter. The course now
runs through Spawell, and through a field called the
coal-field, from traces of coal said to have been found in
it. There was probably a turf-bog here at one time, as
peat is to be seen in the bottom of the deep ditches.
The Tallaght road from Templeogue crosses the course
over an inconveniently steep bridge. This is called the
new road, and was made about 1798. The old road
followed the bank of the Dodder. The course next
works the Templeogue flour-mills, and flows to Kim-
mage.

The principal tributaries to the Dodder in our parish
are—1. A stream rising in Featherbed Bog, behind
Mont Pelier. This passes the curious little valley

between Mont Pelier and the hill behind it, runs
through Piperstown and Friarstown Glen, and joins the
river above Ballinascorney Bridge.

2. A stream rising at the top of the Gap of Ballinascorney ("the town of the gurgling water"). It flows
down that steep, romantic pass, through part of the
old deer-park belonging to Belgard, and, I think,
formerly worked the old parchment-mill. This stream
also ran through part of the extensive deer-park on Mont
Pelier, enclosed by the Conolly family. No doubt,
these deer-parks were well stocked in old times; and it
must have been a grand sight when a meet of the
hounds took place in the beautiful lawn in front of Lord
Ely's hunting-lodge, then surrounded by woods. The
nobles and ladies would take their way up the steep
avenue behind the house, and over the hills, to the glen
at the back of it, under Featherbed Bog. Here they
would probably start some outlying stag, and the chase
would lead over the hills and valleys of Glenasmole,
rivalling the legendary stories of the Finnian hunts
celebrated in old Irish poems. In the steep, narrow
glen through which the Ballinascorney stream flows,
there were formerly some rare ferns to be found, such
as the *Osmunda regalis* and the *Hymenophyllum Tun-
bridgense*. Amateur botanists from Dublin have long
since extirpated every specimen.

3. The third stream has the longest course of any
that here fall into the Dodder. It rises in a small valley
over Johnville, on the side of Tallaght hill, near the old
high road to Blessington. It flows through Johnville
and the lands of Kiltalown, where it is joined by
another small stream, which descends from a valley
above Kiltalown, and is led through some pretty ponds

and waterfalls. The stream bounds the north and west
sides of Kiltalown, on which lands there is a spring of
the purest and coldest water possible. In summer a
glass of it will condense the moisture in the air round it
as if it was iced. This stream passes through Jobstown,
Brooklawn, Whitestown, and again crosses the Tallaght
road. By this time it is a good stream, owing to several
rills that descend from the slopes of the Tallaght hills.
It enters the lands of Old Bawn, where there is a weir
which formerly diverted the principal part of it into a
course of about a mile in length, to the ponds of the
episcopal palace. This weir is of considerable antiquity,
and the stream was used to work the old Manor Mill of
Tallaght at the end of the town. This is all in ruins
now, and the mill-race is so choked with mud and
weeds, that but little water passes through it. Formerly,
after turning the wheel of the Manor Mill, and grinding
all the corn of the tenants—under the usual toll or
mulcture of 1s. a barrel for every barrel not here ground
—part of it was brought across the fields at the back of
Haarlem, by means of deep cuttings and large iron pipes.
There it crossed the parent stream and the tail-race from
Haarlem Mills, down to Boldbrook Mill, where, from
its great purity, it was used in paper-making before
chlorine, China clay, and other bleaching stuffs were
known. It then falls into the Dodder with the tail-race.
This course is long since obliterated, the cuttings filled
up, the iron pipes removed, and so changed are the
fields, that it is scarcely credible that water could have
been brought this way. However, in my young days,
along this very stream there was a short cut from Fir-
House to Tallaght. The only bridges across the stream
were the iron pipes, and it was a hazardous feat for a

young or timid person to walk across them. To return
to the little weir at Old Bawn. Nearly the whole stream
now flows through the fields of Old Bawn, and crosses
the road from Allenton to Tallaght, under the Watergate
bridge. This is rather a recent construction. Formerly
there were stepping-stones and a ford here, and the name
was derived from a gate of the old castle on this side.
A farmer at one time appropriated the stepping-stones
for building his cabin, but the country people made him
replace them. One of these historic stepping-stones is
now lying opposite the forge at the entrance to the
village, near where once stood the celebrated cross of
Tallaght. The stream then flows through some pretty
fields, where a splendid mill-pond might easily be made,
and joins the Dodder mill-race just above the Boldbrook
Mills, after a course of five or six miles.

4. The fourth stream rises to the left of Mont Pelier
House, and flows through a little glen, formerly well
planted, but where now only about twenty trees remain.
There is a little well under an arch, built when the
Long House was erected. It is down in the glen, close
to the stream, and must have been a pretty spot. An
old limekiln, long unused, stands close to it. The stream
crosses the old avenue, and receives another little brook,
rising in a marshy place close by, a sure find for a snipe
or two in winter. It runs then through Old Court, now
the residence of J. Magrane. There was a chapel
here at one time, but only a bit of an ivy-covered wall
remains.

Old Court is mentioned in several early inquisitions
and maps.[1] There are now a substantial farmstead

[1] On the 29th January, 1875, part of the lands of Old Court,
portion of the estate of the Marquis of Ely, were sold, in the
Landed Estates Court, to Mr. William J. Tyndall for £2,060.

and out-offices here, surrounded by a grove of ash trees,
in which there is a large rookery. Before 1828 there
was not a rookery in all this parish, except in the
wood at Templeogue. About that year, a colony established themselves in Sally Park, where there is now a
large rookery. Generally there are from 250 to 300
nests every year. A multitude of starlings also build,
mostly in the same bundle of sticks that the crows
collect for their nests, and in every hollow tree in the
place. After the young birds are fledged, it is pretty to
see the gyrations of the starlings and crows. The
former fly in a compact mass, at great speed, round and
through the crows. These circle about for sometimes
half an hour before settling on their roosts for the
night. The next rookery established was at Old Court.
There is now a thriving colony at Allenton,[1] and another
at Killakee. Near Ballycra the stream is divided by a
small weir : one part is diverted through a deep-covered
drain into Ballycra ; another flows direct through Killininny into the Dodder ; and a third runs through the

[1] This house is built on the site of the ancient church and
monastic establishment of Killininny, or Cill-na-ninghen. These
were founded by the four daughters of MacIaar, who are com-
memorated on October 26th in the Irish Calendar. There are
remains of a castellated building and of a narrow square tower still
to be seen, also some walnut trees supposed to be contempora-
neous with St. Maelruain's tree at Tallaght. At Allenton resided
Sir Timothy Allen, who was in 1762 Lord Mayor of Dublin. In
The Dublin Journal of July 24-27, 1762, it is announced that "last
Saturday evening our worthy Lord Mayor, coming from his country
seat at Temple-Oge, the horse took fright, and ran into a ditch,
by which his lordship was very much cut and bruised ; but we
have the pleasure of assuring the public his wounds are no way
dangerous. His lady, who was in the chaise, received but little
hurt."

walled-in garden of Tymon Lodge. Here is an old-fashioned house, with a curious chimney-stack. The stream supplied an ancient bath-house, about thirty feet by twelve, formerly roofed in, but now in ruins. The garden, too, is now a grass field, with no trace of former cultivation. The stream soon after enters Sally Park, where it supplies the ponds and yards ; and then, flowing through the village of Fir-House, reaches the Dodder just below the weir.

5. The fifth stream rises not far from Killakee upper gate, behind Mount Venus, and, flowing down by Orlagh gate, is joined by a rill that rises very near the top of Mont Pelier, and supplies a pond and fountain in Orlagh. Crossing the road, it flows by the holy well of St. Columkille, then through Ballycullen farm—which has seen better days—and on through Mount Prospect, where were a bath-house and ponds. It now runs through the farmyard of Old Knocklyon, and the lower end of Sally Park, into a fine pond, well stocked with trout, over a waterfall, and on, in a straight course, into the Dodder.

6. The sixth and last stream rises above Woodtown House, on Mount Venus, and, running by a belt of plantation, reaches Beech Park, formerly Sabine Fields. This was once owned by an attorney named Moran, celebrated for having ridden a pony all the way to the Curragh before George IV in 1821. On this occasion several horses of the royal escort dropped dead, from the rapid rate at which it proceeded. Some say His Majesty was afraid of getting a shot. At all events, his splendid horses went at a gallop the whole way. Moran thought much of his pony, which kept ahead the whole time. He was very proud when His Majesty remarked

that it was a good pony.   He had its portrait painted, as
it died after the day's work.

Moran bought at an auction a beautiful group of
figures.   This represented "The Rape of the Sabines."
It included four life-sized figures, cast in metal—those
of a Roman soldier, with a female figure in his arms,
and of two others equally well modelled.   He erected
this on a handsome pedestal in the lawn, where it was
a conspicuous object.   From want of care it fell to
pieces, and the metal was stolen about 1848.   There
were also two grotesque marble figures on the piers of
the gate, representing Nero and Caligula, which have
also long since disappeared.   This place was afterwards
held for some time by a sect of White Quakers, who
established an Agapemone here.   Here they dressed,
men and women alike, in long white robes, and had all
things in common.   The money was put into a wooden
bowl, and each helped himself as he or she needed.   Of
course, this state of bliss could not long continue.   The
establishment was broken up, and the lawyers had some
pickings out of the bottom of the bowl.   This stream
ran through a little wooded glen, where were rustic
bridges and summer-houses, all now gone.   Crossing
part of Ballyroan, the stream formed the boundary of
our parish and of the barony, and joined the Dodder,
through a long tunnel under the road at Pussy's Leap.
For some time past this stream has been brought through
the lands of Ballyroan, and joins the Dodder half a
mile lower down towards Rathfarnham.

These six streams are all those in the parish; owing
to the improved system of drainage, and the quantity of
mountain and marshy land reclaimed, their quantity has
greatly diminished, so that in dry summers many places
are badly off for water.

THE BATTLE OF TALLAGHT.

SHOULD not close this History without giving an account of the Fenian Battle of Tallaght, as it was called, though it was unworthy of the name.

Early in March, 1867, there were rumours of a rising of the Fenians. They had been drilling, and had prepared pikes, guns, and ammunition in the approved style of such rebellions. We were all expecting something to occur. On Tuesday night, the 4th of March, 1867, large bodies of men moved along the Crumlin, Greenhills, Rathmines, and other roads, towards Tallaght. Their object was known to the police, and they were watched. They were not, however, interfered with, as the Government wished them, apparently, to commit some overt act of rebellion. It is not easy otherwise to account for the indifference with which they were allowed to collect arms and organize their forces, while nearly all their affairs being well known to the authorities, by means of paid informers. The indifference or cautiousness of the authorities was carried too far. Had the Fenians succeeded in their first encounter, it is impossible to say how far the insurrection would have extended, or how many lives would have been sacrificed. As it was, several unfortunate men lost their lives in this insensate proceeding. To return to the battle. The small force of police at the various stations were unable or unwilling to attempt any interference with the number

of men who were proceeding, so far, quietly along the
roads. Most of them were decently dressed, and the
very lowest order was unrepresented. At Rathgar, a
party conveying a box of ammunition was challenged
by the police, and ran away, leaving the box behind
them.

The unusual number of strangers passing through
Tallaght in the direction of the hills alarmed the police
at that station. They made what preparations they
could. The barrack was barricaded on the inside, and
messages were sent to the nearest stations to put the
men on the alert. It was soon ascertained that most
of the excursionists were armed, and that a rendezvous
had been appointed on Tallaght Hill.

About midnight, there were only fourteen constables
at the station, under command of Sub-Inspector Burke,
of Rathfarnham, and Head-Constable Kennedy. They
ordered the men to turn out, as the affair was getting
serious. Sub-Inspector Burke and two of the constables proceeded a short way down the road towards
Dublin. They were met by about forty Fenians from
Rathfarnham escorting a cart or van. One of the police
putting his hand into the cart, found it full of cartridges,
cap-boxes, and other ammunition. Chief Burke, as he
was generally called by the country people, called on
the Fenians to surrender. A man, who appeared to be
their leader, replied by attempting to strike one of the
constables with his sword. He immediately drove his
bayonet into the man's body. He fell, and the rest of
the party ran off. They took the wounded man with
them, and left him in a cottage at Balrothery Hill.

The cart was found to contain several hundredweights
of ball-cartridges and percussion-caps, in parcels, boxes,

and packets.   This prize was taken to the barrack.
Soon after, a second party came up from the Greenhills road, who appeared to number four or five hundred.
They advanced to within twenty yards of the police,
who were drawn up near their barrack, which faces the
road.   Chief Burke called on them to surrender in the
name of the Queen; and said that there was a strong
party with him prepared to fire, if his orders were not
obeyed.   The Fenians halted and hesitated.   A few
shots were fired, and a few stones thrown.   Then, as if
panic-stricken, the whole party ran away by the same
road.   The police did not care to follow, as, the night
being dark, they did not know the number of the rebels.

About half-past twelve, another party of about the
same number came along the road from Roundtown.
On being summoned to stand and surrender, they fled
in disorder.

Shortly after a fourth party appeared, coming from the
same direction.   It was made up, as was supposed, of
the runaways from the previous attacks.   They advanced
in military array, and kept step with a precision that
almost deceived the constabulary into the belief that
they were regular soldiers.   The constabulary were
drawn up across the road a few yards from the barrack.
Their orders were to fire at once when the word of
command was given; and they knelt on one knee, ready
to obey.

Sub-Inspector Burke challenged the advancing party,
estimated to have numbered about a thousand.   When
they arrived within twenty or thirty yards of the constabulary, he called on them to surrender in the name of
the Queen, and threatened to fire on them if they did
not lay down their arms.   A person who appeared to be

in command, then cried out, " Here's at it ; now, boys,
now." The words were followed by a volley from the
Fenians. Not a shot took effect, probably from the
kneeling posture of the police. There were about sixty
or eighty shots fired. The constabulary promptly returned the fire, wounding several, and, as it afterwards
appeared, one mortally. The Fenians immediately
turned and fled, throwing away their arms, and leaving
two wounded men on the ground. The police picked
up twelve stands of arms, consisting of rifles, bayonets,
pikes, and daggers, and plenty of ammunition, which
lay scattered about.[1]

Thus ended the much-talked-of Battle of Tallaght.
In this battle a large number of armed and, to some
extent, disciplined Fenians were defeated by fourteen
constables. To Sub-Inspector Burke, for his prompt
action and judicious conduct, great credit is due.

Upwards of 5,000 Fenians collected from other
quarters on Tallaght Hill that night. From some
cause which was not known, the leaders whom they
expected never turned up. The stragglers from the
affray at Tallaght carried to them exaggerated accounts
of the slaughter of their party, and of the capture of
their ammunition. Worse than all, there fell that night
a heavy snow-shower, which quite damped their ardour.
Wet, weary, cold, hungry, and foot-sore, with aching or
quaking hearts, and empty stomachs, the Fenian army

---

[1] About two o'clock on Wednesday morning, Lord Straithnairn,
with a detachment of the 52nd Regiment, some squadrons of the
Scots Greys and Lancers, and a demi-battery of the R.H.A., passed
through Crumlin and Tallaght in pursuit of the Fenians. The
military captured eighty-three, but met with no opposition.—
Freeman's Journal, March 7th, 1867.

broke up, and slunk back to Dublin in small detached parties. They hid their guns, pistols, pikes, and other weapons in every ditch and hedge, being glad to get rid of them in any way. The police captured as many as they pleased. There were no less than sixty-five arrested, and locked up in Tallaght station-house on Wednesday morning. The police also collected seventy boxes of percussion-caps, some hundredweights of bullets, two swords, twenty pike-heads, thirty-two pikes with handles nine and a half feet long, five rifles with bayonets. Subsequently, when the snow melted, great numbers of rifles were found ; and for many months after, revolvers, muskets, and various other weapons were found about the country.

We heard the firing that night, but did not know the cause. Next morning most wonderful stories came in. Numbers of the Fenians had passed through the village outside our wall, and tried to induce the villagers to join them, but with little success.

At my uncle's place at Kiltalown, the family were in a great fright. They saw numbers of Fenians walking about the lawn all night, and they expected to be attacked every moment. All had disappeared by morning ; but in the plantations near the house nearly a cartload of rifles and ammunition was found. Next day we got a fine pike-head and a neat little dagger, as souvenirs of the latest, and, as I hope, the last, rebellion in Ireland.

APPENDICES.

APPENDIX A.

IN MEMORIAM—WILLIAM DOMVILLE HANDCOCK, M.A.

WILLIAM DOMVILLE HANDCOCK was the eldest son of William
Elias Handcock, and was descended from William Handcock, who
came to Ireland with Cromwell's army, and settled at Twyford in
the County Westmeath. He was born on the 2nd September,
1830, and having been educated at Nutgrove School, Rathfarnham,
and at Trinity College, Dublin, took his degree in 1852. He
studied law for some years, and was admitted a solicitor. Afterwards he relinquished the practice of his profession, and became
Dublin agent, with offices at 52 Dame Street, of the Scottish
Union Life Insurance Company, the London and Lancashire Fire
Insurance Company, and the Foreign Passport Office. He
married on the 5th of June, 1862, Ellen Olivier, eldest daughter of
Major Thomas Slator Rooke, of the 12th Madras Light Infantry.
As a magistrate for the County Dublin, Mr. Handcock constantly
presided on the Tallaght Petty Sessions bench, of which he was
a much-valued member. He was also a Guardian of the South
Dublin Union, and a frequent attendant at the meetings of that
board. For many years he was an active supporter of the Society
for the Prevention of Cruelty to Animals. In every kind of charitable work he took a real and practical interest, and his memory
will not soon be forgotten. He was beloved by all who knew him ;
and the death, which occurred on June 5th, 1887, of one so philan-
thropic in character was a loss to many besides his family and
friends.

APPENDIX B.

RESTORATION OF ST. MAELRUAIN'S CHURCH.

THE church of Tallaght was in 1891 restored, and re-opened for Divine Service on November 3rd in that year, by the Archbishop of Dublin, the Most Rev. Lord Plunket. It has been re-pewed, with a wide centre and two side aisles, and the chancel has been raised, panelled with oak, and furnished with choir seats. A handsome carved oak pulpit has been presented. It bears the following inscription:—"Erected by his parishioners and friends in memory of the late Rev. William Robinson, A.M., for fifty-seven years Vicar of this parish. Died November, 1887." The prayer-desk is also of oak. It is inscribed—"In memory of William Domville Handcock, of Sally Park. He entered into rest, June 5th, 1887. Erected by his sorrowing widow and the members of his family." Two painted windows have been placed in the chancel. One, representing "The Sower," has inscribed on it— "To the Glory of God, and in loving memory of the Rev. William Robinson. Born 14th Nov., 1803. Died 9th Nov., 1887. Erected by his children." The other, representing "The Reapers," bears the words—"Gather the wheat into my barn," and was erected, as an inscription below records, "To the Glory of God, and in loving memory of Dorothea, wife of Rev. William Robinson, and Mira and Mary Rebecca, their daughters." A reredos of beautiful workmanship has also been presented. On a brass plate below the Communion rails is the following inscription:—"To the Glory of God, and in loving memory of Evory Kennedy, of Belgard, and Alicia, his wife. This reredos was erected by their children and grandchildren." A stand for the Communion Table has been given "In memoriam, M. R., 1887," and a Bible for the lectern is the gift of Mrs. John Handcock Scott. The total cost of the improvements, which included a new heating apparatus, an American organ, and tesselated pavement, amounted to nearly £1,000.

APPENDIX C.

MURAL TABLETS IN ST. MAELRUAIN'S CHURCH.

East End.

1. Right-hand side.

"Sacred to the memory of Eliza Clancy, who, after a short illness, died on the 8th of January, 1867. Aged 67. She was relict of the late John Clancy, Esq., of Kilnamanagh, in this parish, and daughter of the late Rev. William Whiteside. She was fair in person, affectionate, generous, and sincerely loved by all who knew her. In her latter years she was sorely tried by the death of seven children ; but with pious resignation she looks forward to a glorious reunion, through God her Saviour. Her body lies in the family vault, near the western wall of this church. This tablet is erected as a tribute of the warm affection of her sole surviving and sorrowing brother, Chief Justice Whiteside."

2. Left-hand side.

"They shall walk with me in white, for they are worthy."

"To the deeply loved and honoured memory of Edmond Chomley Farran, who died at Halliford, Middlesex, on Sunday, the 25 Sept., 1881. Aged 34 years."

"We believe that through the grace of the Lord Jesus Christ we shall be saved, even as they." Acts xv. 11.

"Till death us join."

3. Left-hand side.

"To the memory of the Rev. Edward Ryan, D.D., Rector of Donoughmore, in the County of Wicklow, and of St. Luke's, in the City of Dublin. A pious and learned divine. Author of several theological works. He left £500 for the benefit of the poor of his parishes. He died in October, 1818, in the 74th year of his age. This tablet was erected by his nephew, Daniel P. Ryan, Esq., J.P., of Knocklyon, in this parish."

West End.

1. Right-hand side.

"Sacred to the memory of Matthew Handcock, late of Sally Park, County of Dublin, Esquire. He was appointed Deputy Muster

Master-General to his Majesty's Forces in Ireland, in the year 1772 ; which employment he held for a period of fifty years, and until the duties of that department were transferred to the English establishment. His talents and services were justly estimated and remunerated on the reduction of the office. He married in the year 1778, Margaret, daughter of John Butler, Esquire, late first clerk in the office of the Secretary for the Civil Department in Ireland ; by whom he had fourteen children. By judicious and honourable economy, he was enabled to gratify the affectionate and benevolent disposition of his heart towards his numerous relatives, and to provide for his immediate family.

" This tablet was erected by his widow and children as a memorial of their love. Decessit 2do Augusti, A.D. 1824. Deservedly lamented, Margaret, his widow, died 20th March, 1827. Aged 66."

2. Left-hand side.

" In the Family Vault near this lyeth the remains of Margaret M., the dearly loved and affectionate daughter of John and Elizabeth Robinson ; who departed this life, April 5th, 1869. Also John Robinson of Kiltalown, Esq. Died October 11th, 1872, aged 71. Also Elizabeth, his wife. Died June 25th, 1879. " ' For ever with the Lord.' "

3. " In memory of Sir Timothy Allen, Knight, late one of the Aldermen of the City of Dublin. His remains are interred near this place. He died 15 December, 1771. Aged 62 years. His affectionate wife, Lady Jane Allen, caused this tablet to be erected. Also near this place lies interred the body of Miss Elizabeth Isaac."

APPENDIX D.

ANTIQUITIES.

CIST FOUND IN 1898.

MR. GEORGE COFFEY has kindly supplied the following description of the cist, or sepulchral chamber, discovered in a gravel-pit at Greenhills in the summer of 1898 :—

" A cist, measuring about $2\frac{1}{2}$ ft. by 2×2, containing a large burial-urn of hand-made pottery, inverted, and beside it a smaller vessel, upright, was found about 2½ ft. below the surface. The larger urn, when raised, was found to cover cremated bones, among which was a small urn. Dimensions of urns :—(*a*) 12 in. in height; diameter, 10¾ at mouth; 4 in. at base. (*b*) 7½ in. by 6½ and 3⅜. (*c*) 3⅛ by 3⅝ and 1³⁄₁₆.

" A few days later a second interment was found, close to the surface, consisting of a cinerary urn, inverted, over cremated bones. No other urns were with this interment, and it was not in a cist; only a few small flags being placed at the sides. The urn was crushed into fragments, owing to their being no protecting stone over it. The cist and urns first mentioned were removed to the National Museum, and have been set up as found. Their date is about 500 B.C."

A full account will, I believe, be published in the *Proceedings of the R. I. A.*

CINERARY URNS FOUND AT TALLAGHT.

In the *Proceedings of the Royal Irish Academy*, vol. ii, p. 400 (1892), Mr. T. H. Longfield has a drawing of a beautifully decorated cinerary urn which was found on the east side of a hill between Tymon Castle and Greenhills.

The urn was in fragments when found. Its height is 1 foot ½ inch; its greatest diameter, 10½ inches; diameter at mouth, 8¾ inches; and at base, 4½ inches. With it was found a smaller urn or food vessel, a large human skull and arm-bones, and two flint scrapers.

URN FOUND AT KILTALOWN.

In the National Museum is an urn, and fragment of a larger one found in 1848 in the townland of Kiltalown, near the top of the ridge of Tallaght Hill.

No. 93 is a perfect and highly decorated bowl-shaped vessel, probably a food-holder. The ornamentation consists of vertical, horizontal, and wavy lines, with broad fillets intervening, and enriched with impressed markings of a toothed tool; a star and five points on base. Height, 3⅝ in.; diameter of mouth, 5 in.; base, 2¾ in.

No. 94.—The fragment of urn is ornamented with impressed cord-markings.

RATHS.

On the Ordnance Survey map several raths and mounds are marked in this district. Of them Mr. W. P. Briley has given an interesting description, from which most of the following information has been taken:—Raheen Dhu is a large rath with three trenches, and measures 306 feet in circumference; its name is evidently a corruption of Rathin Dubh, from the furze which grows thick and black around it. The country people believe it to be a haunt of the fairies, and say that a house springs up in the middle of the rath, lights stream from the windows, and music is heard all night long. On the top of Cruach Slinn there is a mound, also one behind Mount Seskin House. At Knockanvea is a burial-place; and at Lugmore there is a burial-chamber in the ground, measuring 3 ft. by 2 ft., faced with four stones; its lid, 7 ft. by 5 ft., lies near. It is locally reported that it was discovered by two men, who, on account of a dream one of them had when in Belfast, came to look for treasure. While these men went for help to remove the covering stone, some of the natives raised it, and when the men returned they found only two empty vases. In the neighbourhood it is still firmly believed that these vases were filled with gold, and the place is called the "Treasure Chamber." Probably the vases were some of the cinerary urns already mentioned. At Knockann-vinedee there is also a chamber, surrounded by a circle of stones; at Rathin Bank is a mound. Eugene O'Curry, in his *Ordnance Survey Letters*, calls it an open cairn, and says the Long Stone (Gallan), which Mr. Dix has described, was then standing in a potato field. Much of the stone must be under the surface, as it was higher sixty years ago than it is at present. Near the source of the Dodder is a stone like the top of a cromlech, locally known as the "Shed Stone," having a hollow underneath, one end being much thicker than the other, and supported by a small stone. On the slopes of Glassamucky are several small circles of stones, and the remains of a rath.

APPENDIX E.

SPEAKER CONOLLY.

WILLIAM CONOLLY, who rose to be "the first gentleman" in this kingdom, was a self-made man. His father was an innkeeper in the North of Ireland, probably in the County Donegal, where there was then a strong colony of his name. He was born in 1662. Of his education nothing is known; but the profession which he adopted was that of an attorney. He took the Williamite side in the struggle between William and James, and probably served under Sir Albert Conyngham, ancestor of the Marquis of Conyngham, whose daughter he married. Sir Albert, who had such power in Donegal as to prevent members being elected to James's Parliament from it, lost his life while fighting for King William near Sligo.

Conolly was returned to King William's first Parliament as member for the Borough of Donegal. Shortly after the opening of the Session he was appointed solicitor to the Duke of Ormonde, through the influence of John Ellis, a collateral ancestor of the Agar Ellis family, who was an attached friend of the Ormondes, and held office under several Governments. On the accession of Queen Anne, Conolly was returned as Knight of the Shire for the County of Londonderry, which he continued to represent until his death. He was probably opposed, for he was then, as at subsequent elections, returned also for the pocket-borough of Newtown Limavady, where he had become possessed of a large estate.

He had amassed a great fortune, and owned property in Donegal, as well as in Londonderry, which remained in the possession of the Conollys until recently. In December, 1709, he was appointed a Revenue Commissioner; but in the following September was removed from that office. Swift says that he paid Lord Wharton, the Lord Lieutenant, £3,000 for the appointment; and adds, "So Conolly has made one ill bargain in his life."

In the General Election shortly before the death of Queen Anne, Joshua Dawson, Permanent Secretary at Dublin Castle, contested the County of Londonderry. His opposition was directed against

Conolly's colleague in the representation, Hercules Rowley, ancestor of the Lords Langford. Conolly, at an entertainment which he gave to the voters, " behaved himself very modestly," and did not say one word in favour of Rowley; but Dawson's agent had a shrewd suspicion that he was working for him privately. This subsequent events confirmed, and Conolly and Rowley joined forces as the election drew near. Dawson was defeated. The members' expenses were reported to have amounted to £400—a great contrast to modern election bills, but then thought an incredible sum. Dawson's expenses were some £90.

The burning question of that day was the succession to the Crown. Conolly, who was at the head of the country interest, as it was called, warmly espoused the cause of the Protestant succession, and was in constant communication with the Hanoverian advisers. On the accession of George I, his position was all-powerful. On the one hand, he had the support of the king and of his English Government; on the other, he had gained, by his policy and generous way of living, a great following amongst his own country-men. Thus, when the Speakership fell vacant, on the promotion of Brodrick to the Chancellorship, Conolly was unanimously chosen to take his place.

He was at the same time reinstated as a Revenue Commissioner. When the Lord Lieutenant was about to return to England, Conolly's reputation with the English Government led to his being named as one of the Lords Justices. His appointment gave great offence "to the quality and old gentry," on account of his antecedents. He had also no easy task in succeeding Brodrick in the Speaker's chair, and the impression formed of him during his first Session was that he was unequal to the position.

Soon, however, he raised himself in general estimation. His great wealth was, no doubt, a strong bribe for public favour. His contemporary, Bishop Nicolson, says that his income was one of £12,000 or £13,000 a year; and adds that it was the most valuable which had been raised within memory in Ireland. In political influence he was without rival, and was commonly known as "the great man of the North."

The action of the Duke of Grafton about the famous copper coinage was mainly taken on Conolly's advice; and Swift, in the first of *The Drapier Pamphlets*, gives him a sly hit by pointing out that if the halfpence were allowed to circulate, it would require 250 horses to bring the half-yearly rental of Squire Conolly to Dublin. He purchased, about the end of the seventeenth century, the estate of Castletown, near Celbridge ; and there he built, about the year 1725, the palatial residence which remains a monument to the magnificence and lavishness of his disposition.

On the assembling of the first Parliament of George II, he was again unanimously elected Speaker, but was almost immediately afterwards attacked with serious illness. His condition left no hope of his recovery. He was very unwilling to resign active life ; but finally he was prevailed upon to vacate the Speaker's chair in favour of his friend, Sir Ralph Gore.

Conolly only lived for a few weeks after his resignation, and died on October 29th, 1729. His death was received with loud lamentation and widespread regret. He was compared, as a patriot, with Archbishop King, who had died a short time before; and a sinking nation was said to have beheld with consternation his funeral procession.

He was interred at Celbridge, and his funeral was conducted with much pomp. From his house in Capel Street to the end of Arran Quay, the hearse was accompanied by a great procession on foot. It was headed by the high constable, with a scarf, and six other constables, with hat-bands and gloves, " to clear the way of coaches and any crowds;" then came the beadle of St. Mary's Church, followed by " poor men in black clothes, serge gowns, and hoods, in number sixty-seven, according to his age, each carrying in his hand a pennoncel with the letters of his name and years of his age;" then in succession followed the clerk and sexton of St. Mary's, his porter, footmen, butler, gentleman, and steward, all in cloaks ; various officials ; two gentlemen bearing pennons with his arms ; his surgeon, apothecary, and physicians ; the clergy of St. Mary's; "the minister that inters the corpse ;" the Lord Mayor, Recorder, Aldermen, and Sheriffs, " in their formalities with scarves ;" the clerk of the council ; Athlone Pursuivant, " in his coat," with the helmet and crest ; messengers and doorkeepers of the House of Commons, "bareheaded ; " clerks of the House ; members two-and-two, with scarves ; the chaplain of the House ; the Sergeant-at-Arms and his deputy ; the Speaker, " with a scarf and hat-band ; " Ulster King of Arms, " in his majesties coat with a scarf, with the coat of the defunct's arms ;" the hearse ; the chief mourner ; the other mourners two-and-two, in cloaks ; six privy councillors supporters of the pall ; such of the nobility and gentry "as are pleased to walk two-and-two, with scarves ;" mourning-coaches, "with sets" and pairs ; his Excellency the Lord Lieutenant's coach and six, "with his gentlemen ushers and bed-chambers ;" "coloured" coaches of the nobility and gentry with "sets" and pairs. "For the public benefit of the kingdom," all the scarves—some 700—were of Irish linen, which was then used for the first time instead of silk, and which afterwards became fashionable. At Celbridge a magnificent marble monument, with a long inscription, was erected to his memory by his widow, and remains in perfect preservation to the present day.

Conolly had no children. His widow survived him for more than twenty years, and continued to reside at Castletown, where she built an obelisk and " a wonderful barn," during the years of great famine, to give employment to the poor. Mrs. Delany, in writing to tell her sister of Mrs. Conolly's death, speaks of her as a great and good woman, and gives a long account of her manner of living. Her table was open to her friends of all ranks, and her purse to the poor.

F. E. B.

AUTHORITIES.—*Dictionary of National Biography;* Lodge's *Peerage of Ireland,* by Archdall, vol. vii, p. 180 ; *Journals of the House of Commons ; Brit. Mus., Add. MSS.,* 28, 877, f. 389 ; 21, 122, ff. 86, 88, 90, 91 ; 750 f. 244 ; 6,116, f. 222 ; Scott's *Works of Swift,* vol ii, p. 467, vol. iv, p. 28 ; Craik's *Life of Swift,* p. 349 ; *Primate Boulter's Letters,* vol. i, pp. 163, 265, 267 ; *Letters to and from Bishop Nicolson,* vol. ii, p. 536 ; *Irish Civil Correspondence, Miscellaneous,* Letters from Norman to Dawson in 1713, in Irish Public Record Office ; "Castletown and its Owners," by Lord Walter FitzGerald in *The Journal of the Kildare Archæological Society,* vol. ii, p. 361 ; Elegies on Conolly's death and Order of proceeding to his funeral, amongst Irish pamphlets in Library of Trinity College, Dublin ; *Mrs. Delany's Life and Correspondence,* vol. i, p. 342 ; vol. iii, pp. 138, 166.

APPENDIX F.

DUBLIN AND BLESSINGTON STEAM TRAMWAY.

AN Order in Council was obtained in the year 1880, authorizing
a tramway to be constructed from Terenure to Blessington. About
a mile and a quarter was then laid, on the level of the road, as far
as Templeogue, but the promoters were unable to raise sufficient
capital to continue its construction. In 1887 a baronial guarantee
was obtained, and the construction of a line on a raised platform
was commenced. This line was completed, and opened for traffic
on August 1st, 1888. It runs from Terenure through Templeogue,
Balrothery, Tallaght, Jobstown, and Brittas, to Blessington, the
total length being fifteen and a half miles. It has since been
continued to Poulaphouca Waterfall, four and a half miles from
Blessington, and the extension was opened for traffic in May,
1895.

INDEX.

— ✠ —

C. W. GIBBS & SON, Printers, 18 Wicklow Street, Dublin.